EVERYTHING KO

THE ART OF HOME BREWING, HEALTH BENEFITS, AND CRAFTING UNIQUE FLAVORS WITH COMPREHENSIVE EQUIPMENT AND RECIPE GUIDES

JEFFREY ITO

COPYRIGHT

First Edition

Identifiers: ISBN 9798322950165 (paperback) | ISBN 9798323350636 (hardcover)

Names: Ito, Jeffrey, author.

Title: Everything Kombucha: The Art Of Home Brewing, Health Benefits, And Crafting Unique Flavors With Comprehensive Equipment And Recipe Guides / Jeffrey Ito

DISCLAIMER

The information provided in the books authored by Jeffrey Ito, including but not limited to techniques, recipes, and health benefits of kombucha brewing, is intended for general informational and educational purposes only. Readers should understand that while Jeffrey Ito makes every effort to ensure the accuracy and reliability of the information at the time of its publication, neither the author nor the publishers can accept responsibility for any errors, omissions, or inaccuracies found within these books.

Readers are advised to consult with a qualified health professional before beginning any new dietary practice, especially if they have pre-existing health conditions or concerns. Neither the author nor the publishers shall be liable for any physical, psychological, emotional, financial, or commercial damages, including but not limited to special, incidental, consequential, or other damages.

Opinions and other statements expressed by Jeffrey Ito are his own and are not necessarily endorsed by the publisher or any affiliated entities. Each individual's brewing and consumption experience may vary, and readers are encouraged to exercise their own judgment while engaging with the content provided by Jeffrey Ito.

TABLE OF CONTENTS

CHAPTER 1. PREFACE

Author's Journey with Kombucha

My journey with kombucha began nearly a decade ago, on a brisk autumn morning at a local farmer's market. There, amidst the colorful stalls laden with organic produce, I encountered a small, bubbly sample of something entirely new to my palate—kombucha. It was tart, slightly sweet, and undeniably refreshing. Intrigued by this initial sip and the enthusiastic vendor's tales of its health benefits, I brought home my first bottle of homemade kombucha. That bottle would mark the beginning of an enduring fascination and a journey into the depths of fermenting this remarkable tea.

As someone who has always harbored a passion for nutrition and natural health, kombucha struck a chord with me. It wasn't just the complex flavors that captivated me, but the rich history and the almost alchemical process of fermentation. Eager to delve deeper, I began researching, attending workshops, and eventually brewing my own kombucha. The process was filled with trial and error, learning and discovery. Each batch of kombucha was a testament to the patience and precision required in the art of fermentation.

My kitchen soon transformed into a small laboratory, with jars of brewing tea, various strains of SCOBY, and bottles of experimentally flavored kombucha lining the shelves. The transformation of simple ingredients—tea, sugar, and water—into a probiotic-rich beverage through the natural collaboration of yeast and bacteria was nothing short of magical to me.

Over the years, my hobby grew into a profound commitment. I traveled to meet seasoned brewers, attended international conferences, and connected with a community of kombucha enthusiasts. Each interaction enriched my understanding and appreciation of this drink and its global cultural significance.

Writing this book is a culmination of my adventures with kombucha. It's a sharing of knowledge, from the scientific intricacies of fermentation to the creative joy of flavor experimentation, and an exploration of kombucha's potential health benefits. My goal is not only to guide you through the practical steps of brewing but also to instill a sense of wonder about the cultural tapestry that kombucha weaves across the world.

Through "Everything Kombucha," I invite you to join me on this fizzy journey. Whether you are a curious newcomer or a seasoned brewer, this book aims to nourish your body, delight your taste buds, and inspire your own kombucha journey.

Purpose and Scope of the Book

The purpose of "Everything Kombucha" is to provide a comprehensive guide that demystifies the art and science of kombucha brewing for enthusiasts at all levels. This book aims to be a definitive resource, spanning from the fundamental basics of brewing to the intricate details of flavor creation and health benefits. It is designed to serve not only as a manual for crafting kombucha but also as a deep dive into the cultural, nutritional, and scientific facets of this unique beverage.

The scope of this book covers several key areas:

- **Historical Context**: We explore kombucha's origins and its journey across continents, highlighting how historical uses have shaped its current forms.

- **Scientific Analysis**: Detailed explanations of the fermentation process provide insight into the biochemical reactions that give kombucha its character and health properties. This section is supported by current research on probiotics and their benefits.

- **Practical Brewing Techniques**: Step-by-step instructions, troubleshooting tips, and expert advice equip readers with the tools to brew kombucha confidently at home. This includes setups for beginners and advanced techniques for seasoned brewers.

- **Creative Flavoring and Recipes**: An extensive compilation of flavor combinations and recipes encourages readers to experiment with their brews. This section also includes tips on how to develop unique flavors and use kombucha in various culinary contexts.

- **Health Benefits**: A critical examination of kombucha's health claims versus scientific evidence, discussing its role in a healthy lifestyle.

- **Cultural Impact**: We delve into the social and community aspects of kombucha brewing, including its growth into a global phenomenon and its impact on local economies and cultural practices.

- **Professional and Legal Insights**: For those interested in turning their brewing hobby into a business, this book offers guidance on the commercial aspects of kombucha production, including navigating legalities and marketing.

"Everything Kombucha" is intended to be more than just a cookbook or brewing manual; it is a holistic view of kombucha as a cultural artifact, a health product, and a craft beverage. Whether you are a novice looking to try your first batch or an experienced brewer seeking to refine your technique and expand your knowledge, this book provides valuable insights and practical advice to deepen your understanding and enhance your enjoyment of kombucha.

CHAPTER 2. INTRODUCTION

History and Evolution of Kombucha

The story of kombucha is as rich and effervescent as the drink itself, tracing back over two thousand years. Its origins are steeped in mystery, with numerous tales and folklore surrounding its inception and spread across the world. This section aims to explore the historical journey of kombucha, from its ancient beginnings to its status as a modern-day health elixir.

Ancient Beginnings

Kombucha likely originated in Northeast China around 220 B.C. during the Tsin Dynasty. It was initially prized for its purported health benefits, particularly its detoxifying and energizing properties. The Chinese referred to it as the "Tea of Immortality," a testament to its revered status. The exact recipe and brewing techniques were closely guarded secrets, passed down through generations of healers and herbalists.

Spread Along the Silk Road

As trade routes expanded, kombucha began its journey westward. It traveled along the Silk Road, reaching Russia and Eastern Europe. In these new lands, it was often called "tea kvass" and was popular among the rural folk for its purported health benefits and as a refreshing beverage. Each region adapted the basic kombucha recipe to include local teas and sugar sources, such as beet sugar or honey, reflecting the adaptability and versatility of kombucha brewing.

European Popularity

By the turn of the 20th century, kombucha had become a common household drink in Russia and parts of Germany, where it was valued both for its taste and health benefits. The two World Wars and the Cold War led to a scarcity of tea and sugar, causing a temporary decline in kombucha brewing. However, interest rekindled in the 1960s when Swiss researchers reported that its health benefits were similar to those of yogurt, another fermented product known for its probiotic properties.

Modern Resurgence

The late 20th and early 21st centuries saw a significant resurgence in kombucha's popularity, particularly in North America. Health enthusiasts and alternative medicine practitioners championed kombucha, claiming it could aid a range of conditions from arthritis to heart disease. This period marked the commercialization of kombucha, with numerous brands emerging to cater to a growing consumer base seeking health-oriented products.

The Science and Skepticism

As kombucha grew in popularity, it also attracted skepticism and scientific scrutiny. Research into its probiotic content, antioxidant properties, and potential health benefits increased. While not all health claims have been substantiated by rigorous scientific study, kombucha continues to be studied for its potential metabolic and gut health benefits.

Cultural Impact

Today, kombucha is more than just a health drink; it's a cultural phenomenon. Breweries dedicated to artisanal kombucha are common in many cities around the world, offering a variety of flavors that incorporate local ingredients and brewing traditions. Kombucha festivals, workshops, and brewing clubs have also sprung up, reflecting its role in community building and sustainable living practices.

The history of kombucha is a testament to the human desire for wellness and the cultural transmission of culinary practices. From its mystical origins in ancient China to its modern incarnations as a gourmet health beverage, kombucha has evolved while continuing to fascinate and nourish. Its story is ongoing, with new chapters still being written by kombucha brewers and drinkers worldwide.

What is Kombucha?

Kombucha is a fermented tea beverage that combines tea, sugar, and a symbiotic culture of bacteria and yeast, commonly referred to as a SCOBY (Symbiotic Culture Of Bacteria and Yeast). The fermentation process transforms these simple ingredients into a slightly effervescent drink that is rich in various organic acids, enzymes, and probiotics. This section will break down the components and the fermentation process to provide a clearer understanding of what makes kombucha a unique and popular beverage.

The Basics of Kombucha Composition

1. **Tea**: The base of kombucha is tea—typically black or green, although other varieties can be used. The type of tea influences the flavor and nutrient profile of the final product. The caffeine and polyphenols in tea are crucial for the fermentation process, providing nutrients that feed the SCOBY.

2. **Sugar**: Sugar acts as fuel for the SCOBY, allowing it to grow and ferment the tea into kombucha. While it might seem that kombucha would be overly sweet, most of the sugar is consumed during fermentation, resulting in a final product that is low in sugar.

3. **SCOBY**: The SCOBY is the heart of kombucha brewing. This gelatinous disc is a living colony of bacteria and yeast that works to ferment the sugar-tea solution. The SCOBY consumes the sugar, producing alcohol, carbon dioxide, and various acids,

including acetic, glucuronic, and gluconic acids, which are responsible for the tart, tangy flavor of kombucha.

The Fermentation Process

Kombucha fermentation occurs in two primary stages:

1. **Primary Fermentation**: During this stage, the SCOBY is added to the sweetened tea and left to ferment in a warm environment. This phase typically lasts between 7 to 12 days, depending on temperature and desired acidity. The SCOBY metabolizes the sugar and tea components, producing ethanol and acetic acid, which gives kombucha its distinctive sour taste.

2. **Secondary Fermentation**: This optional stage is for carbonation and flavoring. Once the primary fermentation is complete, the kombucha can be flavored with fruits, herbs, or spices and sealed in an airtight container. This traps carbon dioxide, naturally carbonating the beverage. The secondary fermentation enhances the complexity of flavors and can make the drink more or less acidic, sweet, or fizzy, depending on how long it ferments.

Nutritional and Health Aspects

Kombucha is celebrated for its potential health benefits, primarily attributed to its probiotic content. Probiotics are beneficial bacteria that can help balance the gut microbiome, improving digestion and, potentially, enhancing overall health. Kombucha also contains B vitamins, antioxidants from the tea, and small amounts of minerals and organic acids, which may contribute to its health properties.

However, it is important to approach kombucha with balanced expectations. While many enthusiasts claim that kombucha aids in a variety of health issues from digestive problems to chronic diseases, scientific studies have yet to conclusively back all these claims. As with any fermented food, the benefits of kombucha can vary widely based on the individual, the specific strains of probiotics present, and the method and duration of fermentation.

Understanding what kombucha is, from its basic composition to the complex biochemical processes involved in its production, is essential for both brewers and consumers. This knowledge not only enhances the appreciation of kombucha but also informs healthier and more informed consumption choices. As kombucha continues to grow in popularity, so does our understanding of its potential impacts on health and wellness.

Global Trends and Rising Popularity

Kombucha has transitioned from an ancient elixir to a modern lifestyle beverage, reflecting broader global trends towards health-conscious, sustainable living. This section explores the factors behind the rising popularity of kombucha around the world, the dynamics of its market growth, and its integration into diverse cultures beyond its traditional roots.

Health and Wellness Movement

One of the primary drivers of kombucha's rising popularity is the global shift towards health and wellness. As more people seek natural and holistic approaches to health, kombucha has been embraced as a functional beverage that offers potential health benefits. These include digestive support due to its probiotic content, detoxification properties from its acids, and overall wellness from its antioxidants. This appeal is amplified by growing consumer awareness and education about gut health and the importance of probiotics, making kombucha a go-to choice for those looking to improve their dietary habits.

Craft Beverage Culture

Parallel to the craft beer movement, there has been a surge in craft kombucha production. Artisanal kombucha breweries have sprung up across North America, Europe, and Australia, catering to a clientele that values specialty, locally-sourced, and handcrafted products. These small-scale producers often experiment with a variety of flavors and brewing techniques, pushing the boundaries of traditional kombucha to include a wide range of tastes and styles that appeal to a diverse audience. The craft beverage culture has not only expanded the market but has also elevated kombucha to a trendy lifestyle choice, akin to craft coffee and tea.

Commercial Expansion and Accessibility

Kombucha's transition from niche health food stores to mainstream supermarkets and cafes has significantly boosted its visibility and accessibility. Major beverage companies have entered the kombucha market, either by starting their own lines or by acquiring successful artisanal brands, thus expanding distribution networks globally. This commercial expansion has made kombucha available worldwide, from metropolitan cities to smaller towns, further normalizing its consumption.

Sustainability and Ethical Consumption

In an era where consumers are increasingly concerned about the environmental impact of their choices, kombucha is seen as a sustainable option. The production process is relatively low-impact, often involving organic ingredients and minimal processing. Many kombucha producers also emphasize sustainable practices, such as using recyclable packaging and supporting local tea and sugar farmers. Additionally, the ability to brew kombucha at home reduces waste and carbon footprints associated with commercial beverage production and transport, aligning with the values of environmentally conscious consumers.

Cultural Integration and Global Appeal

As kombucha has spread globally, it has been embraced and integrated into various cultural settings, each adding a unique twist to the traditional brewing process. In Europe, for instance, kombucha is often mixed with locally produced juices to create hybrid beverages. In Asia, innovations include integrating regional tea varieties and sweeteners. This cultural integration has not only increased its appeal across different demographic groups but has also enriched the variety of kombucha available on the market.

The rising popularity of kombucha can be attributed to a confluence of health trends, craft beverage culture, commercial expansion, sustainability concerns, and cultural integration. This diverse appeal ensures that kombucha remains more than just a passing trend but a staple in the global beverage industry. As it continues to evolve, kombucha holds the promise of further innovations and wider acceptance, cementing its place in the dietary habits of people around the world.

The Cultural Significance of Kombucha Across Continents

Kombucha, while rooted in ancient traditions, has woven its way into the cultural fabric of societies worldwide, each adapting it to reflect local tastes and values. This section examines how kombucha has been assimilated into various cultures across continents, highlighting its versatility and the symbolic meanings it has acquired beyond its health benefits.

Asia: The Birthplace and Reinnovation

In China, where kombucha is believed to have originated, it is traditionally consumed for its health benefits, particularly for its supposed longevity-enhancing properties. As kombucha makes a resurgence in modern Asia, it is being rebranded and integrated into contemporary lifestyles, often marketed as a luxury health beverage in urban centers. Innovations include the use of local tea varieties and infusions with native fruits and herbs, aligning with local culinary traditions while appealing to modern tastes and health consciousness.

Russia and Eastern Europe: Traditional Remedies and Household Beverage

In Russia and Eastern Europe, kombucha has a long history as a home remedy and a household beverage, commonly referred to as "tea kvass." It has been traditionally brewed in homes for generations, used both as a daily drink and a medicinal tonic, believed to aid digestion and boost immunity. The cultural practice of home brewing has kept kombucha in the familial and community realm, strengthening social bonds as recipes and SCOBYs are often shared among friends and family.

North America: The Health Revolution and Commercial Boom

Kombucha struck a chord in North America amidst the health and wellness boom. Its fermentation process and probiotic content became highly valued in the context of the rising popularity of gut health. North America leads in commercial kombucha innovation with an array of flavors and brewing techniques that push traditional boundaries. Here, kombucha is not just a beverage but a lifestyle statement, associated with health-conscious, environmentally aware consumers who seek both wellness and taste.

Europe: Artisanal Craft and Sustainable Choice

In Western Europe, kombucha has been embraced within the artisanal food movement, with numerous small-scale producers crafting unique, high-quality kombuchas. European kombucha often features local ingredients, such as regional fruits, herbs, and botanicals, reflecting Europe's rich traditions in craft and natural foods. Moreover, the environmental and sustainable aspects of kombucha production resonate with European consumers who are increasingly focused on ecological impact and ethical consumption.

Australia and New Zealand: Innovation and Flavor Experimentation

In Australia and New Zealand, kombucha has become popular for its perceived health benefits and as a part of the thriving craft beverage scene. Local brands frequently experiment with exotic flavors and innovative brewing methods, such as using native botanicals and even aging kombucha in wine or whiskey barrels for added depth and complexity. This region's approach to kombucha is highly experimental, reflecting a culture that embraces both wellness and culinary innovation.

The cultural significance of kombucha is multifaceted and varies widely across continents. Its ability to adapt to local tastes, traditions, and health beliefs while maintaining its core identity as a fermented health beverage is a testament to its global appeal. As kombucha continues to spread across the globe, it not only adapts to local cultures but also influences them, becoming a part of the social and cultural landscape of countless communities around the world. This cultural adaptability ensures that kombucha remains relevant and continues to evolve with each new generation of brewers and consumers.

CHAPTER 3. THE SCIENCE OF KOMBUCHA

The Biochemistry of Fermentation

The fermentation process of kombucha is a fascinating interplay of biochemistry that transforms simple tea and sugar into a complex, effervescent beverage rich in acids, gases, and bioactive compounds. Understanding the biochemistry of kombucha fermentation not only provides insight into how its distinctive flavors and health benefits are developed but also underscores the intricate relationship between the ingredients and the microbial cultures involved.

Introduction to Fermentation

Fermentation is a metabolic process that converts sugar to acids, gases, or alcohol. In the case of kombucha, this process involves both aerobic and anaerobic steps, primarily carried out by a symbiotic community of bacteria and yeast (SCOBY). This microbial consortium consists mainly of Acetobacter (acetic acid bacteria) and several yeast species, including Saccharomyces and Brettanomyces.

Initial Yeast Activity

The process begins when the SCOBY is introduced to a sweetened tea solution. The yeast components of the SCOBY start the fermentation by breaking down the sucrose into glucose and fructose, a process known as hydrolysis. Yeasts then convert these simpler sugars into ethanol (alcohol) and carbon dioxide (CO_2) through anaerobic respiration, a process known as alcoholic fermentation.

The production of CO2 is what starts to give kombucha its characteristic fizz, although most of the gas is produced later during bottling in the second fermentation phase for commercial kombuchas.

Bacterial Oxidation

As yeast produces ethanol, the bacteria in the SCOBY begin their part of the fermentation. Acetobacter and other acetic acid bacteria oxidize the ethanol into acetic acid under aerobic conditions. This not only gives kombucha its tart, vinegar-like flavor but also contributes to its preservation, as acetic acid is a natural preservative.

Moreover, bacteria convert some of the remaining sugars and alcohols into other organic acids, such as gluconic and glucuronic acids. Gluconic acid contributes to the slightly sweet taste, whereas glucuronic acid is often cited in health discussions for its supposed detoxifying properties, though more scientific research is needed to fully understand its effects in humans.

Formation of Nutritional Components

Throughout the fermentation process, a variety of other beneficial compounds are produced. These include B vitamins, particularly B12, which is produced by certain bacteria, and vitamin C, which results from the metabolic activities of the microbial culture. The tea itself, rich in polyphenols (antioxidants), is transformed, allowing these antioxidants to become more bioavailable—meaning they are easier for the body to absorb and utilize.

The Role of Oxygen

Oxygen plays a crucial role in kombucha fermentation. It is essential for the acetic acid bacteria to perform aerobic respiration. The surface exposure of the kombucha brewing vessel to air is crucial as it facilitates the necessary oxygen intake for these bacteria to thrive and produce acetic acid efficiently.

The biochemistry of kombucha fermentation is a delicate balance between yeast and bacteria, each playing a vital role in transforming the base ingredients into a beverage that is not only unique in flavor but also enriched with potentially beneficial nutrients. The interdependent relationship between these microbes results in a dynamic biochemical environment, leading to the production of a complex array of compounds that contribute to kombucha's distinctive properties. Understanding these processes can help brewers optimize their methods and may provide consumers with greater appreciation for the traditional and scientific craft behind kombucha.

The Anatomy of SCOBY

The SCOBY (Symbiotic Culture Of Bacteria and Yeast) is the heart of kombucha brewing, playing a crucial role in the fermentation process that defines this popular beverage. Understanding the anatomy of the SCOBY is essential for both novice and experienced brewers, as it provides insights into how kombucha's unique flavors and health benefits are developed. This section delves into the composition, function, and care of the SCOBY, shedding light on this fascinating biological entity.

Composition of the SCOBY

A SCOBY is a biofilm or pellicle composed of various microorganisms working in symbiosis. It is primarily made up of cellulose, produced by the bacteria as they consume nutrients from the tea and sugar. This cellulose matrix houses both bacteria and yeasts, forming a thick, rubbery, and somewhat opaque layer that floats on the surface of the kombucha during fermentation.

1. **Bacterial Components**: The bacterial population in a SCOBY is predominantly acetic acid bacteria (AAB), including *Acetobacter*

xylinum and *Gluconacetobacter kombuchae*. These bacteria are responsible for converting ethanol produced by the yeasts into acetic acid, contributing to the vinegar-like taste of kombucha. They also produce the cellulose that forms the physical structure of the SCOBY.

2. **Yeast Components**: The yeasts in a SCOBY are typically from the genera *Saccharomyces*, *Brettanomyces*, *Pichia*, and others. These yeasts ferment the sugars from the sweetened tea to produce ethanol and carbon dioxide. The carbon dioxide contributes to the effervescence of the kombucha, while the ethanol is a critical substrate for the acetic acid bacteria.

Function of the SCOBY

The SCOBY acts as a bio-reactor, facilitating the conversion of sweet tea into kombucha through a series of biochemical reactions:

1. **Sugar Fermentation**: Yeasts in the SCOBY break down the sucrose into glucose and fructose, which are further metabolized into ethanol and carbon dioxide.

2. **Acid Production**: The acetic acid bacteria convert the ethanol into acetic acid, lowering the pH of the kombucha, which not only flavors the beverage but also helps preserve it by inhibiting the growth of unwanted pathogens.

3. **Synthesis of Nutritional Compounds**: The microbial activity in the SCOBY also leads to the synthesis of various other acids, vitamins, and enzymes that contribute to the purported health benefits of kombucha.

Care and Maintenance of the SCOBY

Proper care and maintenance of the SCOBY are vital for successful kombucha brewing:

1. **Optimal Conditions**: The SCOBY performs best in a controlled environment with temperatures ranging from 68 to 78 degrees Fahrenheit (20 to 26 degrees Celsius). It requires a neutral-to-acidic pH environment, which is naturally maintained in the kombucha fermentation process.

2. **Handling and Storage**: The SCOBY should be handled with clean hands and tools to prevent contamination. Between batches, it can be stored in a small amount of kombucha liquid in a cool, dark place. The liquid, often referred to as "starter tea," helps maintain the SCOBY's health and provides a medium rich in nutrients.

3. **Regeneration and Multiplication**: After each batch, the SCOBY typically thickens as new layers form on top of the old. These layers can be separated gently to propagate new SCOBYs for additional batches or to share with others.

The SCOBY is not only a fascinating example of symbiosis but also the critical component in the production of kombucha. Understanding its composition and functions helps brewers optimize their fermentation processes and achieve the desired taste and quality in their kombucha. Proper care and handling of the SCOBY ensure that it remains healthy and active, capable of producing high-quality kombucha batch after batch.

Health Claims vs. Scientific Evidence

Kombucha has been celebrated for its purported health benefits, ranging from digestive support to disease prevention. However, the enthusiasm around these claims often outpaces the scientific evidence available. This section critically examines the health claims associated with kombucha by comparing them with the scientific evidence to provide a balanced perspective.

Common Health Claims of Kombucha

1. **Digestive Health**: Kombucha is often touted for its probiotic content, which is believed to improve gut health by promoting a healthy balance of gut flora. Probiotics are known to aid digestion and boost the immune system.

2. **Detoxification**: Supporters claim that kombucha helps detoxify the body, particularly the liver. This is attributed to glucuronic acid, a compound purportedly present in kombucha, which is known to conjugate with toxins to facilitate their excretion.

3. **Immune System Boosting**: The beverage is believed to strengthen the immune system due to its high antioxidant content, particularly from tea polyphenols, and vitamin C.

4. **Joint Health**: Kombucha contains glucosamines, which are compounds claimed to help maintain collagen and prevent joint degeneration.

5. **Energy Enhancement**: The presence of B vitamins and small amounts of caffeine from the tea are said to provide an energy boost.

Reviewing the Scientific Evidence

1. **Digestive Health**: The probiotic content of kombucha can indeed support gut health; however, the types and concentrations of probiotic strains in kombucha can vary greatly depending on the fermentation process. Not all kombucha products may contain beneficial levels of live probiotics, and commercial pasteurization can reduce their efficacy.

2. **Detoxification**: There is limited scientific evidence supporting the claim that kombucha can detoxify the body. While glucuronic acid is involved in detoxification in the liver, there is little evidence that the glucuronic acid in kombucha is available in a form that the body can use for this purpose.

3. **Immune System**: While kombucha contains antioxidants from tea, the extent to which these antioxidants can boost the immune system is not well-documented in scientific literature. The overall impact may be positive but should not be overstated.

4. **Joint Health**: The evidence linking kombucha consumption to improved joint health is anecdotal. While glucosamines are known to be beneficial for joint health, the concentration in kombucha is generally low and likely insufficient to have a therapeutic effect.

5. **Energy Enhancement**: The energy-boosting effects of kombucha are primarily due to its caffeine and B vitamins content, which can indeed contribute to increased energy levels. However, the amounts are typically small and vary between batches.

While kombucha can be a healthful addition to the diet, providing benefits similar to those of other fermented foods, the scientific evidence does not fully support many of the broader health claims made by proponents. Consumers should enjoy kombucha for its taste and general benefits associated with fermented foods, such as probiotic content, while maintaining realistic expectations about its medicinal capabilities. As with any supplement or health food, kombucha should be consumed as part of a balanced diet and not relied upon as a cure-all. Further research is needed to clarify its role in health and to substantiate the specific health claims often associated with it.

Safety and Health Risks

While kombucha is consumed by many with positive effects, like any food product, especially those that are fermented, it carries potential safety and health risks that consumers should be aware of. This section addresses the primary concerns associated with kombucha consumption, providing information to ensure safe brewing and consumption practices.

Contamination Risks

1. **Pathogenic Microorganisms**: The open fermentation process of kombucha can sometimes allow harmful bacteria or molds to contaminate the SCOBY and the brew. Consuming contaminated kombucha can lead to health issues such as food poisoning, nausea, vomiting, and diarrhea.

2. **Proper Sanitation**: To mitigate this risk, it is crucial to maintain strict hygiene and sanitation standards during the brewing process. This includes using sterilized equipment, clean working environments, and ensuring that the SCOBY does not show signs of mold growth, which appears as green, black, or orange fuzzy spots.

Alcohol Content

1. **Variable Alcohol Levels**: During fermentation, yeast converts sugars into ethanol (alcohol). The alcohol content in home-brewed kombucha can sometimes exceed the expected levels, potentially reaching up to 3% alcohol by volume (ABV) or higher, depending on fermentation time and conditions.

2. **Regulation and Consumption**: In many countries, beverages with an alcohol content above 0.5% ABV must be labeled as alcoholic. Consumers, particularly those who avoid alcohol for health, religious, or recovery reasons, should be cautious and possibly use home testing kits to determine alcohol content.

Acidity

1. **High Acidity**: Kombucha is naturally acidic, with pH levels usually between 2.5 and 3.5. Consuming highly acidic beverages can lead to dental erosion or gastrointestinal discomfort in some individuals.

2. **Managing Consumption**: It is advisable to consume kombucha in moderation and to possibly rinse the mouth with water after drinking kombucha to help protect tooth enamel.

Unpasteurized Kombucha

1. **Health Risks**: Unpasteurized kombucha contains live cultures of bacteria and yeast, which can pose risks to pregnant women, infants, the elderly, and individuals with compromised immune systems, due to the potential presence of harmful microorganisms.

2. **Advisory**: Health experts typically recommend that at-risk groups avoid consuming unpasteurized fermented products to prevent any potential infections or health complications.

Homemade vs. Commercial Kombucha

1. **Consistency and Safety**: Commercial kombucha is generally brewed in controlled environments and is subject to food safety regulations, which helps ensure consistency in alcohol content, acidity, and cleanliness. Home-brewed kombucha, while offering customization and potentially greater probiotic diversity, varies more in these aspects and requires careful monitoring to maintain safety.

The popularity of kombucha must be balanced with awareness and caution, particularly when it comes to home brewing. While many enjoy kombucha without adverse effects, understanding the potential safety and health risks is crucial. By adhering to rigorous sanitation practices, monitoring fermentation conditions closely, and being mindful of consumption habits, kombucha can be safely enjoyed as part of a healthy diet.

CHAPTER 4: EQUIPMENT AND SETUP FOR HOME BREWING

Choosing the Right Equipment

For those interested in home brewing kombucha, selecting the right equipment is crucial for ensuring a successful fermentation process and achieving the desired quality of the beverage. This section provides a comprehensive guide to the essential equipment needed for brewing kombucha at home, covering everything from fermentation vessels to bottling supplies.

Fermentation Vessels

1. **Type of Container**: Glass is the most recommended material for brewing kombucha because it is non-reactive and does not leach chemicals into the brew, unlike certain plastics or metals. Ensure that the glass is clear and not colored, as transparency allows for better monitoring of the fermentation process.

2. **Size and Shape**: The size of the vessel depends on the quantity of kombucha you plan to brew. A common size for home brewers is a 1-gallon (approximately 3.8 liters) jar, which provides ample space for the SCOBY to grow and facilitates easy handling. Wide-mouth jars are preferable as they provide more surface area for oxygen exchange and make it easier to insert and remove the SCOBY and other ingredients.

3. **Covers**: The top of the fermentation vessel should be covered with a breathable material, such as a tight-weave cloth, coffee filter, or paper towel, secured with a rubber band. This cover keeps out contaminants like dust and insects while allowing air to circulate.

Temperature Control

1. **Thermometer**: Maintaining the correct temperature is vital for optimal SCOBY activity. A stick-on thermometer attached to your fermentation vessel can help you monitor the temperature, which should ideally be between 68-78 degrees Fahrenheit (20-26 degrees Celsius).

2. **Heating Mats**: In cooler environments, a heating mat specifically designed for fermentation can help maintain a consistent temperature. Ensure that the heat is evenly distributed and that the setup does not overheat the kombucha.

pH Testing

1. **pH Meter or Test Strips**: Testing the pH of your kombucha helps ensure it is within the safe and optimal range (typically between 2.5 and 3.5) for fermentation. pH meters provide more accuracy, but test strips are a more economical option.

Brewing and Measuring Tools

1. **Measuring Cups and Spoons**: Accurate measurement of ingredients like sugar and tea is essential for consistent results. Use non-metallic measuring tools to avoid any reaction with kombucha's acidity.

2. **Wooden or Plastic Stirring Utensils**: Metal utensils should be avoided when stirring kombucha as they can react with the acidic environment. Wooden spoons or plastic stirrers are safe alternatives.

Bottling Supplies

1. **Bottles**: Bottles for storing kombucha should be glass and capable of sealing tightly to allow for carbonation during the secondary fermentation. Swing-top bottles are popular for their ease of use and good seal.

2. **Funnel and Strainer**: A plastic funnel and a non-metal strainer are useful for transferring kombucha into bottles while filtering out any tea residue or pieces of SCOBY.

Cleaning and Sanitization

1. **Non-Abrasive Cleaners**: It's important to keep all brewing equipment clean and free from residues. Use hot water and vinegar or a non-abrasive, food-safe cleaner to wash all equipment before and after use.

2. **Sanitizer**: Sanitizing all equipment before use can be done with diluted food-grade sanitizer solutions to ensure that no unwanted bacteria contaminate the brew.

Choosing the right equipment for brewing kombucha is a foundational step in the home brewing process. By selecting appropriate materials and tools, you can ensure a safe and efficient brewing environment that produces high-quality kombucha. Always prioritize cleanliness and precision to foster the best conditions for your kombucha fermentation.

Creating a Home Brewery Setup

Establishing a dedicated space for brewing kombucha at home can enhance the efficiency of your brewing process and help maintain the quality and safety of your kombucha. This section will guide you through the steps to create an optimal home brewery setup, focusing on location, organization, and environmental conditions.

Choosing the Right Location

1. **Temperature Control**: Select a location in your home where the temperature can be consistently maintained between 68-78 degrees Fahrenheit (20-26 degrees Celsius). Avoid places with wide temperature fluctuations, such as near heating vents, windows, or exterior doors.

2. **Low Light**: Kombucha cultures best in a space that is away from direct sunlight. UV rays can inhibit the growth of the SCOBY and affect the fermentation process. A cupboard, pantry, or a shaded corner of the kitchen or basement can provide an ideal environment.

3. **Ventilation**: While direct airflow like drafts should be avoided as they can introduce contaminants and cool the brewing area, some ventilation is beneficial to prevent any buildup of mildew or mold in the brewing area, especially if it's in a more confined space.

Organizing Your Space

1. **Storage for Supplies**: Set up shelving or storage space to organize your tea, sugar, SCOBYs, pH meters, thermometers, and other brewing necessities. Keeping your supplies organized and within reach will streamline your brewing process and ensure cleanliness.

2. **Work Area**: Ensure there is a clean, flat surface area where you can prepare the tea and sugar mixture, handle the SCOBY, and bottle your kombucha. This area should be easily cleanable, preferably not directly on wood or other porous surfaces that could harbor bacteria.

3. **Safety First**: Make sure your brewing area is away from pets and young children to avoid accidental contamination and ensure that the environment remains undisturbed.

Environmental Conditions

1. **Cleanliness**: Maintaining a clean brewing environment is crucial. Before setting up your brewery, thoroughly clean the area with non-toxic cleaners and keep it free from dust and debris. Regularly clean the space before and after each brewing session.

2. **Avoiding Contaminants**: Keep the brewing area free of plants, flowers, or fruit bowls, as these can harbor insects or mold spores

that could contaminate the kombucha. Additionally, if using a shared space like a kitchen, be mindful of cooking fumes and smoke, which can also alter the quality of your brew.

Brewing Vessel Placement

1. **Stable Surface**: Ensure that your fermentation vessels are placed on a stable surface where they won't be jostled or knocked over. Vibration or movement can disturb the formation of the SCOBY and affect the fermentation.

2. **Accessibility**: Place the vessel at a height that is easy to access for regular checks and tasting but secure enough to prevent any accidental tipping. The location should also facilitate easy cleaning around and underneath the vessel.

Tools and Equipment

1. **Dedicated Tools**: Have a set of tools dedicated solely to kombucha brewing, including measuring spoons, cups, funnels, and stirrers. This prevents cross-contamination with other cooking tools and ingredients.

2. **Labeling**: Clearly label all ingredients and tools, and keep a logbook or brewing diary to track each batch's progress, including dates, ingredient amounts, pH levels, and temperatures. This can help refine your process and troubleshoot any issues.

Creating a home brewery for kombucha is about more than just finding space—it's about creating a controlled environment that promotes the health and vitality of your SCOBY and yields delicious kombucha. By carefully considering the location, organizing your supplies, and controlling the environment, you can set up a home brewery that is both functional and enjoyable, leading to consistent and rewarding brewing results.

Importance of Sanitation

Sanitation is one of the most crucial aspects of kombucha brewing. A clean brewing environment and sterile equipment are essential to ensure the health of your SCOBY and the safety of your kombucha. Proper sanitation practices prevent contamination by unwanted bacteria, yeasts, or molds, which could spoil your kombucha and potentially cause health issues. This section outlines the key practices for maintaining optimal sanitation throughout the kombucha brewing process.

Understanding the Risks

1. **Contamination**: The biggest threat in kombucha brewing is contamination from pathogens, mold, and spoilage organisms. These contaminants can outcompete the SCOBY's microbial community or introduce toxins into the brew, making it unsafe for consumption.

2. **Cross-Contamination**: Using equipment that is also used for other kitchen tasks can introduce foreign microbes into your kombucha. This can alter the fermentation dynamics or introduce harmful bacteria.

Sanitation Best Practices

1. **Cleaning and Sterilizing Equipment**: Before each use, all brewing equipment, including fermentation vessels, measuring cups, funnels, and bottles, should be thoroughly cleaned and then sterilized. You can clean with hot, soapy water followed by rinsing with clean, hot water. For sterilizing, options include using a diluted vinegar solution, non-scented bleach solution (properly diluted), or commercially available food-safe sanitizers. Rinse any cleaned and sanitized equipment with hot water to remove any residual cleaning agents.

2. **Preparing the Brewing Area**: The area where you brew and bottle your kombucha should be as clean and free from dust and debris as possible. Wipe down surfaces with a food-safe sanitizer and maintain a tidy environment to minimize the risk of airborne contaminants settling in your kombucha.

3. **Handling the SCOBY**: Always wash your hands thoroughly before handling the SCOBY or any ingredients that will come into contact with your kombucha. Consider wearing clean disposable gloves when handling the SCOBY to minimize direct contact and potential contamination.

4. **Use of Proper Coverings**: Cover your fermenting kombucha with a tightly woven cloth, coffee filter, or paper towel secured with a rubber band. This barrier should be dense enough to keep out contaminants but porous enough to allow air to circulate, which is essential for the fermentation process.

5. **Monitoring for Contamination**: Regularly check your kombucha and SCOBY for signs of mold or unusual smells. Mold typically appears as green, black, white, or orange fuzzy spots on the surface of the SCOBY or kombucha. If you detect any mold, discard the SCOBY and the kombucha immediately, as mold can produce dangerous toxins that are not safe to consume.

6. **Maintaining pH Levels**: Keeping the kombucha at the correct pH level (below 4.5, typically around 2.5 to 3.5) is also a safety measure, as it creates an acidic environment that inhibits the growth of harmful bacteria.

Maintaining stringent sanitation practices is not just about ensuring the quality and taste of your kombucha; it's about safeguarding your health and the health of those who share your brew. While the process might seem rigorous, establishing good habits from the start makes sanitation second nature and ensures that your kombucha brewing experience is both successful and enjoyable. With cleanliness as a priority, you can brew with confidence, knowing that your kombucha is not only delicious but also produced in a safe and controlled environment.

Initial Cost and Maintenance

Setting up a home brewery for kombucha can be an exciting endeavor, but it's important to consider both the initial investment and ongoing maintenance costs to ensure sustainable and enjoyable brewing. This section breaks down the typical expenses associated with starting and maintaining a home kombucha brewing setup.

Initial Costs

1. **Fermentation Vessel**: A high-quality glass fermentation vessel is essential. Costs can range from $20 for a basic 1-gallon jar to $100 or more for larger, more specialized containers like stainless steel vessels designed for brewing.

2. **SCOBY and Starter Tea**: A healthy SCOBY with starter tea typically costs between $10 and $30, depending on the source. It's possible to obtain a SCOBY for free from another brewer or to grow your own from a commercial bottle of raw kombucha, which could also be a cost-effective option.

3. **Tea and Sugar**: The raw materials for brewing, primarily tea and sugar, are relatively inexpensive. Bulk purchases of organic tea leaves and sugar can help reduce these costs further. Expect to spend about $5 to $10 per batch, depending on the quality and source of ingredients.

4. **Bottling Supplies**: Bottles for storing kombucha, especially those with airtight seals suitable for carbonation, can vary in price. A set of six 16-ounce glass bottles typically costs between $10 and $30. Reusing bottles from store-bought beverages can also be a cost-saving measure.

5. **Measuring and Testing Equipment**: Basic tools like a kitchen scale, measuring cups, and pH test strips or a pH meter are

necessary. These can cost anywhere from $5 for basic strips to $50 for a reliable digital pH meter.

6. **Heating Equipment**: Depending on your climate, a heating mat or belt may be necessary to maintain optimal fermentation temperatures. These typically range from $20 to $60.

Ongoing Maintenance Costs

1. **Ingredient Restocking**: Regular purchases of tea and sugar are the primary ongoing cost. Buying in bulk can reduce the per-batch cost significantly.

2. **SCOBY Care**: While the SCOBY can last indefinitely with proper care, occasionally it may need to be replaced due to aging or contamination. This might incur an additional cost if a new SCOBY needs to be purchased.

3. **Cleaning Supplies**: Investing in non-toxic cleaners or sanitizers for equipment maintenance is a minor but regular cost. Alternatively, household items like vinegar can be used effectively and are more cost-efficient.

4. **Energy Consumption**: If using a heating mat, the additional energy consumption can add to your utility bills, although this cost is generally minimal.

5. **Replacement of Equipment**: Over time, you may need to replace or upgrade certain elements of your brewing setup, such as bottles or the fermentation vessel, due to wear and tear or to enhance the brewing process.

Budgeting Tips

• **Start Small**: Begin with a basic setup to minimize initial costs. You can upgrade components as you become more experienced and committed to the hobby.

- **DIY Solutions**: Consider DIY alternatives, such as building your own fermentation box or using repurposed bottles and jars.

- **Bulk Purchases**: Buy ingredients and sanitizing supplies in bulk to reduce the per-unit cost.

- **Energy Efficiency**: Opt for energy-efficient heating solutions and only use them as necessary to keep costs down.

Understanding the initial and ongoing costs of kombucha brewing helps in planning and budgeting for your home brewery. While the start-up investment can be relatively modest, the actual enjoyment and potential health benefits of home-brewed kombucha can provide substantial value. With careful planning and smart shopping, brewing kombucha at home can be both economically feasible and immensely rewarding.

Chapter 5: The Brewing Process: A To Z

Preparing the Ingredients

Proper preparation of ingredients is a critical first step in the kombucha brewing process. This section will guide you through selecting and preparing the tea, sugar, and water necessary to create a successful kombucha batch.

Selecting the Tea

1. **Type of Tea**: Kombucha can be brewed with various types of tea, but the most commonly used are black and green teas due to their nutrient content and flavor profiles. The type of tea can significantly impact the taste and health properties of the final product. Herbal teas can also be used, either alone or blended with black or green tea, but avoid teas with essential oils, such as Earl Grey, which can harm the SCOBY.

2. **Organic vs. Non-Organic**: Organic teas are preferred by many brewers because they are free from pesticides and other chemicals that could potentially harm the SCOBY and alter the flavor of your kombucha.

3. **Loose Leaf vs. Bagged**: Loose leaf tea is generally superior in quality compared to tea bags and allows for better extraction of flavors and nutrients. However, tea bags can be more convenient and are perfectly acceptable if they are of high quality.

Choosing the Sugar

1. **Type of Sugar**: Plain white cane sugar works best for kombucha brewing as it is easily broken down by the yeast during

fermentation. Organic cane sugar is a popular choice for those seeking a more natural product.

2. **Alternatives**: While white sugar is standard, some brewers experiment with other sugars like raw sugar, honey (which changes the brew to "jun kombucha"), maple syrup, or agave. These can alter the flavor and effectiveness of fermentation, so they should be used with caution and perhaps after some experience with standard recipes.

3. **Amount**: The amount of sugar will depend on the recipe, but it typically ranges from ¾ to 1 cup per gallon of water. It's important to measure accurately because the sugar is not just for sweetness but primarily serves as food for the SCOBY.

Preparing the Water

1. **Quality of Water**: Use clean, filtered water if possible. Chlorinated tap water can inhibit the SCOBY and should be avoided. If filtered water is not available, let tap water sit out overnight to allow chlorine to evaporate or boil it for 10 minutes and then cool it before use.

2. **Temperature**: The water should be heated to the appropriate temperature to steep the tea—usually between 175°F and 212°F (79°C to 100°C), depending on the type of tea. Green tea requires cooler water (about 175°F) to prevent bitterness, while black tea can handle boiling water (212°F).

Brewing the Tea

1. **Steeping Time**: Steep the tea for about 5 to 10 minutes, depending on how strong you want the tea flavor to be. Longer steeping times result in a stronger tea, which can provide a more robust flavor base for the kombucha.

2. **Cooling**: After steeping, the tea must be cooled to room temperature before adding the SCOBY. Adding the SCOBY to hot tea can kill it or significantly inhibit its activity.

3. **Straining**: If using loose leaf tea, strain the leaves from the tea using a fine mesh strainer to prevent them from altering the texture or clarity of the final kombucha.

The preparation of kombucha ingredients is not just a routine step but a foundational one that sets the stage for successful fermentation. Each ingredient—from the type of tea and sugar to the quality of water—plays a significant role in the flavor, health benefits, and overall quality of the kombucha. Properly prepared ingredients ensure that the SCOBY has the best environment to thrive and produce delicious kombucha.

The Step-by-Step Guide to First Fermentation

The first fermentation is where the magic of kombucha brewing begins. This stage is crucial as it sets the foundation for the flavor and quality of your kombucha. Here's a detailed step-by-step guide to ensure you successfully navigate through the first fermentation process.

Step 1: Prepare the Sweet Tea

1. **Boil Water**: Start by boiling the appropriate amount of water for your batch. For a standard 1-gallon batch, you'll need about 13-14 cups of water.

2. **Add Tea**: Once the water is boiling, remove it from the heat and add your tea. Use about 8-10 tea bags or 2-3 tablespoons of loose leaf tea per gallon of water.

3. **Steep Tea**: Allow the tea to steep until it has completely infused the water, typically about 5 to 10 minutes, depending on the strength desired.

4. **Dissolve Sugar**: While the tea is still hot, add the sugar and stir until completely dissolved. The typical ratio is 1 cup of sugar per gallon of water.

5. **Cool the Mixture**: Allow the sweet tea to cool to room temperature (68-78 degrees Fahrenheit). This is crucial to avoid harming the SCOBY.

Step 2: Add the SCOBY and Starter Tea

1. **Prepare Vessel**: Ensure your fermentation vessel is thoroughly cleaned and sanitized.

2. **Transfer Tea**: Pour the cooled sweet tea into your fermentation vessel.

3. **Add Starter Tea**: Add about 2 cups of starter tea per gallon of sweet tea. This helps to acidify the brew, creating an environment that is protective against harmful pathogens.

4. **Place SCOBY**: Gently place the SCOBY on top of the liquid in the vessel. If it sinks, don't worry; it will still ferment properly.

Step 3: Cover and Store

1. **Cover the Vessel**: Cover the top of the fermentation vessel with a clean, tightly woven cloth (like muslin or a coffee filter) and secure it with a rubber band. This cover allows air in but keeps contaminants out.

2. **Store Properly**: Place the vessel in a warm (68-78 degrees Fahrenheit), dark place where it won't be disturbed. Avoid direct sunlight and drastic temperature changes.

Step 4: Fermentation Duration

1. **Ferment**: Let the kombucha ferment for about 7 to 30 days. The duration will depend on your taste preferences and the

temperature of the brewing environment. Warmer conditions typically speed up the fermentation process.

2. **Taste Test**: Start tasting the kombucha after about 7 days by gently inserting a straw beneath the SCOBY to draw a small sample. The right taste is subjective but generally, kombucha should have a slightly sweet and tangy flavor. If it's too sweet, it may need more time to ferment.

Step 5: Monitor and Adjust

1. **Monitor SCOBY**: Check periodically to ensure your SCOBY is healthy. A healthy SCOBY is thick, light-colored, and free of mold. Dark strands or patches are typically yeast and not a concern, but green, black, or orange spots may indicate mold.

2. **Adjust Storage**: If you notice the fermentation is going too slowly, you may need to find a warmer spot or consider using a heating mat to maintain a consistent temperature.

The first fermentation phase is primarily about transforming sweet tea into tangy, slightly sweet kombucha through the action of the SCOBY. By carefully managing the ingredients, temperature, and time, you can create a delicious base that's ready for further flavoring in the second fermentation or enjoyed as is. Remember, patience is key; each batch can vary, and part of the joy of brewing kombucha is discovering the unique character of each fermentation cycle.

Techniques for Successful Second Fermentation

The second fermentation (F2) of kombucha is where you can get creative with flavors and achieve that delightful carbonation that many enjoy. This stage is optional but highly recommended for those looking to enhance their kombucha's taste and effervescence. Here's how to master the second fermentation:

Step 1: Preparation for Flavoring

1. **Choose Your Flavors**: Decide on the flavors you want to add. Common additions include fresh fruits, herbs, spices, and juices. Think about the combinations that might work well, like ginger and lemon, raspberry and mint, or apple and cinnamon.

2. **Prepare Flavor Ingredients**: Depending on what you're using, prepare your additions. For fruit, you might puree it, chop it finely, or use it as juice. Herbs and spices should be fresh or whole for the best infusion.

3. **Quantity of Flavors**: The amount of flavoring ingredients can vary, but a general guideline is to use about 10-20% of the volume of your kombucha. For instance, for a one-liter bottle of kombucha, you might add 100-200 ml of juice or fruit puree.

Step 2: Bottling

1. **Prepare Bottles**: Ensure your bottles are clean and sanitized. Bottles should be glass and capable of sealing tightly, as pressure will build up inside them.

2. **Remove the SCOBY**: Before you bottle the kombucha for its second fermentation, carefully remove the SCOBY along with about a cup of kombucha from your fermentation vessel to use as the starter for your next batch.

3. **Add Flavorings**: Distribute your prepared flavorings into the bottles. You can use a funnel to make this process cleaner and easier.

4. **Fill with Kombucha**: Pour the kombucha into the bottles over the flavorings, leaving about an inch of headspace at the top to allow room for the carbon dioxide that will form.

Step 3: Secondary Fermentation

1. **Seal the Bottles**: Cap the bottles tightly to ensure no gas can escape. This is crucial for developing carbonation.

2. **Store Bottles**: Place the bottles in a dark, room-temperature spot to ferment for anywhere from 3 to 14 days. The exact time will depend on the temperature and how fizzy you want your kombucha to be.

3. **Burp Bottles**: Check the pressure in the bottles every day or two by briefly opening them to release any excess gas ("burping"). This prevents bottles from exploding due to over-pressurization.

Step 4: Monitoring and Storage

1. **Taste Test**: After a few days, begin tasting your kombucha by carefully opening one of the bottles. If it has reached your desired level of carbonation and flavor, it's ready to be refrigerated.

2. **Refrigerate to Stop Fermentation**: Once your kombucha is carbonated to your liking, move the bottles to the refrigerator. This halts the fermentation process and preserves the flavor and carbonation level.

Step 5: Serving

1. **Strain if Necessary**: If you've used chunks of fruit or herbs, you might want to strain the kombucha as you pour it into a glass to remove any solid pieces.

2. **Enjoy Chilled**: Serve your flavored kombucha chilled for the best taste experience.

The second fermentation of kombucha allows you to customize the flavor and enhance the sensory experience of your brew. With careful attention to the type and amount of additions, along with proper bottling and storage techniques, you can create delicious, naturally carbonated kombucha at home. Always remember safety first: keep an eye on the pressure build-up in the bottles to avoid any accidents.

Monitoring Fermentation Progress

Successfully brewing kombucha involves closely monitoring its fermentation progress to ensure the desired balance of sweetness, acidity, and effervescence. This section provides a guide on how to effectively track the changes in your kombucha during the fermentation process, allowing you to make adjustments as needed and achieve consistent results.

Understanding Fermentation Stages

1. **Initial Activity**: In the first few days of fermentation, you might not see much visible activity. The SCOBY will begin to metabolize the sugars, and you may notice a slight cloudiness forming in the tea.

2. **Active Fermentation**: After a few days, you should start to see signs of active fermentation, such as bubbles forming around the SCOBY and possibly the surface of the liquid. The SCOBY may float at the top or sink to the bottom—either is normal.

3. **Acidification**: As the fermentation progresses, the kombucha will start to smell vinegary due to the production of acetic acid. This is a good sign that the fermentation is proceeding correctly.

Daily Observations

1. **Visual Checks**: Look for signs of mold or unusual changes in the SCOBY's appearance. Mold can appear fuzzy and is usually green, white, black, or blue. Any presence of mold means you should discard the entire batch, including the SCOBY, to avoid health risks.

2. **Smell Tests**: Sniff your brew daily. It should start to develop a pleasantly sour smell. A foul or rotten odor is a warning sign of contamination or a bad fermentation process.

Measuring Progress

1. **pH Testing**: Using pH strips or a digital pH meter, regularly check the pH of your kombucha. The ideal pH for finished kombucha is between 2.5 and 3.5, indicating sufficient acidification for safe consumption and good flavor balance.

2. **Taste Testing**: Begin tasting your kombucha after about a week of fermentation by gently inserting a straw beneath the SCOBY, covering one end with your finger to draw up some liquid. The kombucha should taste slightly sweet and tangy. If it's too sweet, allow it to ferment for a few more days.

Adjusting Fermentation

1. **Temperature Adjustments**: If fermentation seems slow, it may be too cold. Consider moving your brewing vessel to a warmer location or using a heating mat. Conversely, if the kombucha is fermenting too quickly or tastes overly acidic, try a cooler spot.

2. **Time Adjustments**: The length of fermentation time can be adjusted based on your flavor preferences. Longer fermentation times will result in less sweetness and more vinegar-like tartness.

Record Keeping

1. **Maintain a Log**: Keep a fermentation log to record the start date, pH levels, temperature, taste observations, and any adjustments made during the process. This record-keeping will help you replicate successful batches and understand more about your personal preferences and the variables affecting your brew.

Monitoring the fermentation progress of your kombucha is vital for crafting a high-quality beverage. By paying close attention to visual cues, smells, pH levels, and taste, you can ensure the health of your SCOBY and the safety and flavor of your kombucha. Adjustments based on careful monitoring can greatly improve your results, making your home-brewed kombucha a delightful and rewarding endeavor.

Chapter 6: Advanced Techniques and Professional Tips

Mastering Temperature and pH Control

In the art of kombucha brewing, achieving the perfect balance of flavor and ensuring the safety of the brew often come down to precise control of temperature and pH. These factors play critical roles in the fermentation kinetics, microbial health, and overall quality of the final product. This section provides advanced techniques and professional tips for mastering temperature and pH control during kombucha brewing.

Temperature Control

1. **Ideal Temperature Range**: The optimal temperature range for kombucha fermentation is between 68-78 degrees Fahrenheit (20-26 degrees Celsius). Temperatures within this range encourage a balanced fermentation rate, promoting both yeast and bacterial activity essential for developing depth in flavor and ensuring efficient conversion of sugars into acids and other beneficial compounds.

2. **Maintaining Consistent Temperature**:

    - **Heating Mats**: In cooler climates or during colder months, heating mats can be used to maintain a stable temperature. Place the mat under the brewing vessel and monitor the temperature closely to avoid overheating.

    - **Cooling Methods**: During hot weather, place the fermentation vessel in the coolest part of your house, such as a basement, or use a small fan or periodic air conditioning to prevent temperatures from rising above the upper threshold.

- **Thermal Wraps**: Insulating the fermentation vessel with a thermal wrap can help stabilize the temperature by minimizing the impact of external temperature fluctuations.

3. **Monitoring Tools**: Use a digital thermometer or a temperature sticker attached to your fermentation vessel for continuous monitoring. Frequent checks and adjustments ensure that the kombucha is fermenting under optimal conditions.

pH Control

1. **Importance of pH**: The pH of kombucha should be monitored to ensure it falls within a safe and effective range. Initially, your kombucha will start at a higher pH level (around 4.5 to 5.0) and should drop below 4.0 within a few days to prevent harmful bacterial growth. The target finishing pH is typically between 2.5 and 3.5, where kombucha has developed its characteristic tartness and is microbiologically stable.

2. **Measuring pH**:

- **pH Strips**: Simple and cost-effective, pH strips can provide a quick estimate of the pH level. However, they may not offer precise readings.

- **Digital pH Meters**: For more accuracy, especially when dialing in specific flavor profiles or for commercial production, a digital pH meter is recommended. Calibrate the pH meter regularly to ensure accuracy.

3. **Adjusting pH**:

- **Early Fermentation Adjustments**: If the pH does not drop below 4.0 naturally within the first few days, it may be necessary to add a small amount of distilled white vinegar to lower the pH and secure a safe fermentation environment.

- **Balancing Flavor and Safety**: Towards the end of fermentation, if the kombucha is too tart, adjusting the length of fermentation time or the sugar content in future batches can help modulate acidity.

Professional Tips

1. **Batch Notes**: Keep detailed notes on temperature and pH readings along with any adjustments made during each batch. This documentation can help refine your process and achieve consistent results.

2. **Microbial Health**: Monitor the health and thickness of your SCOBY. A healthy SCOBY is indicative of a well-maintained brew environment. Signs of thinning or discoloration could suggest issues with temperature or pH balance.

3. **Consistency Over Batches**: Achieving consistency in flavor and quality across batches heavily relies on the precise control of environmental factors, especially temperature and pH. Experiment with small adjustments to develop a deeper understanding of how each factor affects your kombucha.

Mastering the control of temperature and pH in kombucha brewing enhances both the safety and the sensory qualities of your beverage. By implementing these advanced techniques and maintaining vigilant monitoring, brewers can elevate their kombucha from a homemade experiment to a refined, consistent craft product.

Experimentation with Hybrid Teas

Exploring hybrid teas in kombucha brewing offers a unique opportunity to diversify flavor profiles and tap into the subtleties of tea blending. This section provides insights and guidance on how to successfully incorporate hybrid teas into your kombucha brews, enhancing both complexity and nuance in the final product.

Understanding Tea Blending

1. **Basics of Hybrid Teas**: Hybrid teas involve blending two or more different types of tea leaves to create a unique flavor, aroma, and chemical composition. The goal is to balance the strengths of each tea type to produce a harmonious end result that offers depth and complexity.

2. **Choosing Teas**: When selecting teas for blending, consider their individual characteristics:

   - **Black Tea**: Offers robustness and depth, with higher caffeine content and strong tannins.

   - **Green Tea**: Provides subtle flavors and lower tannin levels, with a gentle, often grassy or floral taste.

   - **White Tea**: Delicate and light, contributing sweetness and mild flavors.

   - **Oolong Tea**: Ranges from light to full-bodied, with floral to woody notes, depending on oxidation levels.

   - **Herbal Teas**: Add specific flavors and medicinal qualities but lack the nutrients needed for fermentation, so they should be used in combination with a camellia sinensis base (black, green, or white tea).

Techniques for Blending

1. **Start Small**: Begin with small quantities and simple blends. For instance, mixing a robust black tea with a fragrant green tea can balance the strength of the black tea with the aromatic qualities of the green tea.

2. **Ratio Experimentation**: Experiment with different ratios to find the ideal balance. A common starting point is a 50/50 blend, adjusting based on which tea characteristics you want to emphasize.

3. **Taste As You Go**: Brew small test batches of your hybrid tea blend as a regular tea before adding it to your kombucha to gauge flavor and strength. Adjust the blend based on your taste preferences and the desired outcome for the kombucha.

Brewing with Hybrid Teas

1. **Adjust Fermentation Variables**: Different teas may ferment at different rates due to varying nutrient and tannin contents. Monitor the fermentation process closely and be prepared to adjust fermentation times and temperatures accordingly.

2. **Monitor pH and Flavor Development**: Hybrid teas can alter the typical pH progression and flavor development of your kombucha. Use pH testing and regular tasting to guide the fermentation process, ensuring the brew does not become too acidic or bitter.

3. **Document Changes**: Keep detailed records of the types of teas used, their proportions, and the resulting flavor profiles. This documentation will be invaluable for replicating successful blends and refining less successful ones.

Advanced Tips

1. **Seasonal Blends**: Consider creating seasonal tea blends that complement the time of year, such as lighter, floral teas for spring or richer, spicier teas for autumn.

2. **Cultural Fusions**: Experiment with teas from different cultural backgrounds to create unique, fusion-inspired kombucha flavors. For example, a blend of Japanese sencha and Indian Assam could yield a kombucha that is both earthy and bold.

3. **Aging Potential**: Some tea blends may develop deeper flavors over time. Consider aging these kombucha brews longer than usual to enhance their characteristics.

Experimentation with hybrid teas in kombucha brewing not only broadens the flavor spectrum but also enhances the artisanal quality of the beverage. By carefully selecting, blending, and testing teas, brewers can achieve a distinctive kombucha that stands out in both complexity and taste. This creative endeavor requires attention to detail and an openness to continuous learning and adaptation.

Long-Term Fermentation Methods

Long-term fermentation of kombucha can lead to a more complex flavor profile, increased acidity, and potentially enhanced probiotic content. This section explores advanced techniques for extending the fermentation period, providing practical advice for brewers seeking to experiment with longer brew cycles.

Understanding Long-Term Fermentation

1. **Basics of Extended Fermentation**: In long-term fermentation, kombucha is allowed to ferment beyond the typical 7 to 30 days. This extended period can range from several weeks to several months, during which the kombucha continues to acidify and mature in flavor.

2. **Effects on Kombucha**: As the fermentation duration increases, the sugar content decreases, and the acidity increases. The flavor profile shifts towards a more vinegary taste, and the drink typically becomes less sweet and more tart. Additionally, the microbial dynamics may change, potentially increasing the diversity and concentration of beneficial bacteria.

Preparing for Long-Term Fermentation

1. **Choose the Right Container**: For long-term fermentation, use a container that allows minimal air exchange to prevent

contamination and excessive evaporation. Glass containers with airlock lids are ideal as they allow gases to escape while keeping contaminants out.

2. **Maintain a Healthy SCOBY**: Ensure that the SCOBY is healthy and robust before beginning a long-term fermentation. A thicker, more mature SCOBY is typically more resilient and capable of sustaining longer fermentation periods.

3. **Adjust the Sugar Content**: Consider increasing the initial sugar content slightly to sustain the yeast over the extended fermentation period. However, be cautious not to add too much, as this can disrupt the balance and lead to overly sweet or excessively alcoholic kombucha.

Monitoring and Maintenance

1. **Regular Checks**: Regularly inspect the kombucha for signs of contamination, such as mold or off smells. If contamination occurs, the batch should be discarded to avoid health risks.

2. **pH Monitoring**: Keep track of the pH throughout the fermentation. Long-term fermented kombucha should gradually reach a pH of around 2.5 to 3.5. pH below 2.5 may be too acidic for enjoyable consumption and could potentially damage the SCOBY.

3. **Taste Testing**: Periodically taste the kombucha to gauge its flavor development. This will help you decide when it has reached your preferred flavor profile or if it should ferment longer.

Potential Risks and Considerations

1. **Over-Acidification**: Prolonged fermentation can lead to very high acidity, which might not only make the kombucha unpleasant to drink but also inhibit the SCOBY's ability to function effectively.

2. **SCOBY Health**: Over time, the SCOBY may become too acidic and start to degrade. Regularly renew your SCOBY from fresher batches to maintain a healthy culture.

3. **Evaporation**: Over longer periods, evaporation can concentrate the kombucha and alter its flavor and acidity. Top off with fresh tea or cover the vessel more securely to minimize evaporation.

Advanced Techniques

1. **Continuous Brewing**: Instead of brewing in batches, consider a continuous brewing system where fresh sweet tea is added periodically to replace the kombucha that has been drawn off. This method can maintain a more consistent and manageable acidity level and allows for regular harvesting of kombucha at different stages of fermentation.

2. **Flavor Adjustments**: For overly tart kombucha, blend it with freshly brewed, sweeter kombucha to balance the flavor or add fruit juices or herbs during a secondary fermentation phase to enhance the flavor profile.

Long-term fermentation is a method suited for those who appreciate a more pronounced tartness and complexity in their kombucha. By carefully managing the fermentation environment, monitoring the health of the SCOBY, and being attentive to the evolving taste and acidity, brewers can develop a uniquely robust kombucha. This advanced brewing technique rewards patience with depth of flavor and potentially greater health benefits.

Achieving Consistency in Batch Brewing

Consistency is a hallmark of skilled kombucha brewing, especially when producing multiple batches. Achieving a consistent quality, flavor, and effervescence in every batch can be challenging due to the natural variations in the biological processes involved.

This section provides essential techniques and tips to help you maintain consistency across your kombucha brews.

Understanding the Variables

1. **Ingredients**: The quality and proportions of tea, sugar, and starter tea can significantly affect the outcome. Ensure that you use the same type and quality of ingredients in the same proportions for each batch.

2. **SCOBY Health**: The health and age of your SCOBY play critical roles in how effectively it ferments the tea. A healthy SCOBY ensures a robust and stable fermentation process.

3. **Environmental Factors**: Temperature and humidity levels can vary widely and influence the speed and character of fermentation. Consistent environmental conditions are key to consistent kombucha.

Standardizing the Process

1. **Recipe and Ratios**: Keep a precise recipe and stick to it. Use a digital scale for measuring ingredients to ensure accuracy, and always measure your ingredients the same way.

2. **Fermentation Vessel**: Use the same type of fermentation vessel for each batch. Material (glass, stainless steel), size, and shape can affect how the kombucha ferments.

3. **Fermentation Time**: Keep a consistent fermentation schedule. Starting with similar pH levels and tasting your kombucha regularly can help you decide the exact right time to end the fermentation for consistent flavor.

4. **Documentation**: Keep detailed records of each batch, including the type of tea, amount of sugar, fermentation duration, temperature logs, and tasting notes. This documentation will be invaluable for troubleshooting and fine-tuning future batches.

Controlling Environmental Conditions

1. **Temperature Control**: Maintain a consistent brewing temperature within the optimal range (68-78 degrees Fahrenheit). Use a heating mat or a cooler location as needed depending on seasonal changes.

2. **Avoid Contamination**: Always sanitize your equipment thoroughly before starting a new batch. Contamination can introduce unwanted variables that affect the taste and safety of your kombucha.

Quality Control Measures

1. **pH Monitoring**: Regularly use pH strips or a digital pH meter to monitor the acidity of your kombucha, ensuring it falls within the desired range before bottling.

2. **Taste Testing**: Develop a consistent tasting schedule. By tasting at the same point in the fermentation process, you can better gauge when each batch has reached its optimal flavor profile.

3. **SCOBY Rotation**: Rotate out older SCOBYs and introduce fresh ones periodically. Older SCOBYs can accumulate yeast imbalances or become less effective over time.

Implementing Consistency in Scaling Up

1. **Batch Sizing**: When increasing the volume of your kombucha production, make proportional adjustments to ingredients and closely monitor the scalability of environmental control, particularly temperature.

2. **Multiple Vessels**: If using multiple fermentation vessels, ensure they are all in the same environment and manage each vessel's microenvironment as closely as possible.

Achieving consistency in kombucha batch brewing is about meticulous control and standardization of the brewing process and conditions. By focusing on the precision of your ingredients, the health and maintenance of your SCOBY, and the stability of your brewing environment, you can produce consistently high-quality kombucha. Remember, even with all these measures, some variation is natural and can be embraced as part of the unique character of home-brewed kombucha.

CHAPTER 7: FLAVOR INNOVATION AND RECIPE DEVELOPMENT

The Science of Flavoring Kombucha

Flavoring kombucha is both an art and a science, allowing brewers to customize their brews with a wide array of tastes and aromas. Understanding the science behind flavoring can help enhance the kombucha experience, making each batch both delicious and unique. This section delves into the fundamentals of kombucha flavoring, exploring how various ingredients interact with the base brew during the second fermentation.

Basic Principles of Kombucha Flavoring

1. **Flavor Absorption**: During the second fermentation, kombucha continues to ferment, absorbing flavors from added ingredients. This process not only infuses flavor but can also affect the overall acidity and sweetness of the final product.

2. **Volatility of Flavors**: Some flavors are more volatile than others and may dissipate quickly if not properly captured during the fermentation process. The timing of adding these flavors and the conditions under which they are fermented can significantly impact their presence in the final brew.

3. **Interaction with Acids**: The acidic environment of kombucha can alter the flavor profile of added ingredients. For example, certain fruity flavors might become sharper or more pronounced, while others may mellow out.

Selecting Ingredients for Flavoring

1. **Fruits**: Common choices include berries, citrus, apples, and tropical fruits. These can be added in various forms such as fresh, frozen, dried, or as juices. Each form offers different intensities and complexities of flavor.

2. **Herbs and Spices**: Adding herbs and spices can create depth and complexity. Commonly used herbs include mint, basil, and lavender. Spices like ginger, cinnamon, and clove are popular for adding warmth and spice.

3. **Other Additives**: Some brewers explore using floral notes like hibiscus or rose petals, and even unconventional ingredients like coffee or chocolate, to create distinctive flavors.

Techniques for Adding Flavors

1. **Timing of Additions**: Adding flavorings during the second fermentation allows the flavors to meld with the kombucha without being overwhelmed by the ongoing fermentation processes that dominate the first stage.

2. **Preparation of Ingredients**: The preparation of flavoring ingredients affects their integration into the kombucha. For example, finely chopping or muddling fruits can expose more surface area to the brew, enhancing flavor extraction. Steeping spices or herbs can similarly intensify their impact.

3. **Quantity and Ratios**: The amount of flavoring added can vary depending on the desired intensity of the flavor and the type of ingredient used. It's generally recommended to start with small quantities and adjust based on taste. Typically, about 10-20% of the total volume in flavoring agents is sufficient.

Managing Flavor During Fermentation

1. **Controlling Fermentation Time**: The length of the second fermentation affects flavor intensity. Longer fermentation can

lead to more pronounced flavors but also increases acidity, which may not be desirable with certain delicate flavors.

2. **Temperature Control**: The fermentation temperature can influence not only the rate of fermentation but also the development of flavors. Warmer temperatures generally accelerate fermentation and flavor development.

3. **Taste Testing**: Regular taste testing during the second fermentation is crucial to ensure that the flavors develop as expected and do not become overpowering or unbalanced.

Flavoring kombucha offers endless possibilities to customize and enhance the beverage according to personal preferences. By understanding the science of how different flavors interact with the base kombucha and mastering the techniques of flavor addition, brewers can craft a superior product that delights the palate with every sip. This exploration of flavor not only improves the brewing skill but also deepens the appreciation for the complexity and versatility of kombucha.

Recipes for Beginner, Intermediate, and Advanced Brewers

Expanding your kombucha brewing skills through a variety of recipes can cater to different levels of brewing experience. This section provides curated recipes tailored for beginner, intermediate, and advanced kombucha brewers, enabling each to experiment with new flavors and techniques suited to their skill level.

Beginner Recipe: Simple Ginger Lemon Kombucha

Ingredients:

- 1 gallon of plain kombucha (first fermentation completed)

- 1 large lemon

- 2 inches of fresh ginger root

Instructions:

1. **Prepare Flavorings**: Thinly slice the lemon and ginger. No need to peel the ginger, but wash it thoroughly.

2. **Add to Kombucha**: Distribute the lemon slices and ginger evenly among the bottles.

3. **Second Fermentation**: Seal the bottles and let them ferment at room temperature for 2-4 days. Check daily for desired carbonation and flavor.

4. **Refrigerate**: Once the flavor and fizziness are to your liking, refrigerate to stop fermentation.

5. **Serve**: Strain the kombucha when pouring into glasses, if desired, and enjoy!

This recipe is perfect for beginners due to its simplicity and the robust flavors that are hard to get wrong.

Intermediate Recipe: Blueberry Vanilla Kombucha

Ingredients:

- 1 gallon of plain kombucha (first fermentation completed)

- 1 cup fresh or frozen blueberries

- 1 vanilla bean, split lengthwise, or 1 teaspoon pure vanilla extract

Instructions:

1. **Prepare Blueberries**: If using fresh blueberries, lightly mash them to release their juice. If using frozen, allow them to thaw first.

2. **Add to Kombucha**: Place blueberries and vanilla bean or extract into your fermentation bottles.

3. **Second Fermentation**: Seal the bottles and let them ferment for 3-5 days, checking periodically for flavor development and carbonation.

4. **Refrigerate**: Chill the bottles to stop fermentation once the desired flavor intensity and carbonation are achieved.

5. **Serve**: Enjoy your flavor-rich kombucha straight from the fridge.

This recipe introduces the technique of using vanilla and the challenge of balancing the subtle flavors of berry and vanilla.

Advanced Recipe: Lavender Chamomile Kombucha

Ingredients:

- 1 gallon of plain kombucha (first fermentation completed)

- 1/4 cup dried lavender flowers

- 1/4 cup dried chamomile flowers

- Honey or sugar syrup to taste (optional, for added sweetness)

Instructions:

1. **Prepare Infusion**: Create a strong infusion by steeping lavender and chamomile in a cup of boiling water for about 10 minutes. Strain the infusion and let it cool.

2. **Add to Kombucha**: Add the cooled herbal infusion to your kombucha along with honey or sugar syrup if using.

3. **Second Fermentation**: Bottle the kombucha with the infusion and seal tightly. Allow fermenting for 5-7 days, tasting regularly to monitor the development of the flavors.

4. **Refrigerate**: Once you're satisfied with the taste and fizziness, move the kombucha to the refrigerator.

5. **Serve**: Serve chilled for a relaxing and refined drink.

This advanced recipe requires managing the subtle and delicate flavors of herbs, monitoring their infusion, and balancing sweetness and tartness.

Each recipe offers a different level of complexity and introduces new skills and flavors. As you progress from beginner to advanced brewing, these recipes not only enhance your palate but also expand your brewing techniques, encouraging creativity and mastery in the art of kombucha making.

How to Create and Test New Flavors

Creating and testing new flavors in kombucha brewing is an exciting way to personalize your brews and explore a broader spectrum of sensory experiences. This section offers a step-by-step guide on how to innovate with new flavors, from conceptualization to execution, ensuring that your experiments are both creative and successful.

Step 1: Conceptualization

1. **Inspiration**: Draw inspiration from your favorite foods, drinks, or seasonal ingredients. Consider combinations that are popular in culinary arts, such as pairing fruit with herbs (e.g., strawberry and basil) or exploring regional flavors (e.g., tropical fruits for a Caribbean twist).

2. **Research**: Look into flavor profiles that might complement the natural tartness of kombucha. Citrus, berries, and stone fruits are traditionally successful, but also consider more adventurous additions like spices, floral notes, and even vegetables.

3. **Goal Setting**: Decide what you want to achieve with your new flavor. Are you looking for something refreshing, soothing, or perhaps a flavor that could pair well with meals? Setting a clear goal will help guide your experimentation.

Step 2: Preparation

1. **Ingredient Selection**: Choose high-quality, fresh ingredients for the best flavor extraction. If you're using herbs or spices, consider whether fresh or dried forms would work best for the intensity of flavor you're aiming for.

2. **Small Batches**: Start by preparing small test batches. This allows you to experiment with different ratios and combinations without wasting large amounts of ingredients if the batch does not turn out as expected.

3. **Documenting Recipes**: Keep a detailed record of what you add to each batch, including the type, quantity, and preparation of each ingredient.

Step 3: Experimentation

1. **Flavor Infusions**: Add your chosen flavors to the kombucha during the second fermentation phase. This is when the kombucha is bottled and can develop carbonation and enhanced flavors from the added ingredients.

2. **Variations**: Don't hesitate to create multiple small variations of your flavor idea by adjusting the amounts of each ingredient or how they are prepared (e.g., chopped, juiced, whole).

3. **Testing Variables**: Along with different ingredients, test variables like fermentation time and temperature, as these can significantly impact the flavor outcome and intensity.

Step 4: Evaluation and Refinement

1. **Taste Testing**: Organize regular tasting sessions every day or two during the fermentation to monitor the development of flavors. It's helpful to involve others in these sessions for a broader range of feedback.

2. **Sensory Notes**: Take notes on not just the taste but also the aroma, mouthfeel, and appearance of each test batch. This comprehensive sensory evaluation can help refine the flavor to achieve the desired profile.

3. **Adjustments**: Based on feedback, make adjustments to the recipe. This might involve increasing the concentration of an ingredient, extending the fermentation time, or tweaking the preparation method of the ingredients.

Step 5: Finalizing and Scaling Up

1. **Select the Best Version**: Once you've refined the recipe through several small batches, select the version that best meets your goals and has the desired sensory attributes.

2. **Scale Up**: Gradually scale up the production of your new flavor to larger batches, ensuring that the flavor consistency holds true in larger volumes.

3. **Continuous Improvement**: Even after finalizing a recipe, there's always room for improvement. Continue to seek feedback and make small adjustments to perfect the flavor over time.

Creating and testing new flavors in kombucha is an iterative and creative process that enhances the brewing experience and can lead to unique, customized brews. By systematically experimenting with different combinations and carefully documenting and refining the results, you can develop signature kombucha flavors that stand out in taste and quality.

Pairing Flavors with Food

Pairing kombucha with food is an artful endeavor that enhances the dining experience by complementing or contrasting flavors that elevate both the meal and the beverage. This section will guide you through the principles and strategies for successfully pairing kombucha flavors with various types of food, turning each meal into a harmonious culinary adventure.

Understanding Flavor Profiles

1. **Balance**: The key to successful flavor pairing is balance. Kombucha inherently possesses a complex profile—tart, sweet, and sometimes bitter. Understanding and balancing these with the flavors of your dishes is crucial. For instance, a sweet kombucha can balance a dish with spicy elements, whereas a tart kombucha might pair well with fatty or rich foods.

2. **Complementing**: Choose kombucha flavors that complement the dominant flavors of your dish. For example, a berry-flavored kombucha goes well with a dessert like chocolate cake or a fruit-based dish.

3. **Contrasting**: Alternatively, select a kombucha that provides a contrast to the main flavors of the meal, such as pairing a ginger-lemon kombucha with a seafood dish to cut through the richness and refresh the palate.

Pairing Strategies

1. **Rich and Creamy Dishes**: Foods that are rich and creamy can be beautifully balanced by kombucha with bright acidity or a hint of sweetness. A mango or peach-flavored kombucha can cut through the richness of dishes like creamy pasta or a rich curry.

2. **Spicy Foods**: Spicy dishes pair well with sweet or fruity kombuchas as they help soothe the heat. Pineapple or passionfruit

kombucha can be an excellent match for spicy Asian or Latin dishes.

3. **Grilled or Smoky Flavors**: Smoky flavors from grilled meats or barbecued dishes are complemented by kombuchas with earthy or smoky notes, such as an oolong tea kombucha or one infused with smoked herbs.

4. **Light and Fresh Dishes**: Salads or light fish dishes pair well with subtle, delicate kombucha flavors like cucumber mint or chamomile.

5. **Desserts**: Sweet desserts are a perfect match for kombuchas with bold, fruity, or spicy flavors. A cinnamon apple kombucha can complement apple pie beautifully, while a chocolate-infused kombucha could pair with creamy desserts.

Practical Pairing Tips

1. **Taste Testing**: Always taste your kombucha alongside the dish to see how the flavors interact. This can help you adjust the seasoning of the dish or choose a different kombucha if necessary.

2. **Seasonal Pairings**: Consider the season when pairing food and kombucha. A summer meal might call for a lighter, more refreshing kombucha, while winter dishes could be paired with a richer, deeper-flavored kombucha.

3. **Cultural Themes**: Align the kombucha pairing with the cultural theme of the meal. For instance, a kombucha with green tea and lychee would go well with Asian dishes, while a kombucha infused with citrus and rosemary might suit Mediterranean food.

Hosting and Presentation

1. **Serving Suggestions**: Serve kombucha in wine glasses or champagne flutes to elevate the dining experience and make it more engaging.

2. **Guest Preferences**: Always consider the preferences of your guests; some may prefer a less acidic or milder kombucha. Offering a variety of kombucha flavors can be a thoughtful way to accommodate different palates.

Effectively pairing kombucha with food not only enhances the flavors of both but also introduces an element of culinary sophistication to your meals. By understanding and applying the principles of flavor balance, complementation, and contrast, you can create memorable dining experiences that showcase the versatility and delightful complexity of kombucha.

CHAPTER 8: NUTRITIONAL INSIGHTS AND HEALTH BENEFITS

Probiotic Benefits: A Detailed Look

Kombucha is celebrated not only for its unique taste but also for its probiotic properties, which contribute to various health benefits. This section provides an in-depth examination of the probiotic benefits of kombucha, explaining how these live microorganisms contribute to gut health and overall wellness.

Understanding Probiotics in Kombucha

1. **What are Probiotics?**: Probiotics are live microorganisms that, when consumed in adequate amounts, confer a health benefit on the host. In the context of kombucha, these are primarily lactic acid bacteria that can survive the acidic environment of the gut and may help balance the gut microbiome.

2. **Sources of Probiotics in Kombucha**: During fermentation, the SCOBY (Symbiotic Culture Of Bacteria and Yeast) metabolizes the sugars in the tea to produce not only alcohol and acetic acid but also several strains of health-promoting bacteria and yeast. The exact composition of these microorganisms can vary significantly between batches, depending on factors like the SCOBY's origin, the tea used, and fermentation conditions.

Health Benefits of Probiotics

1. **Digestive Health**: Probiotics in kombucha can help restore the balance of gut flora, which is crucial for healthy digestion. This balance aids in breaking down food and absorbing nutrients more efficiently. Regular consumption of kombucha might help

alleviate common digestive issues like bloating, constipation, and diarrhea.

2. **Immune System Support**: The gut microbiota plays a critical role in the immune system by protecting against pathogens and maintaining overall immune health. Probiotics from kombucha can strengthen the gut barrier, reducing the risk of infections and potentially enhancing immune responses.

3. **Mental Health**: Emerging research suggests a link between gut health and mental health, often referred to as the "gut-brain axis." Probiotics in kombucha may help improve mood and cognitive functions, potentially alleviating symptoms of depression and anxiety.

4. **Metabolic Benefits**: Some studies suggest that probiotics can influence weight, cholesterol levels, and overall metabolic processes. By improving gut health, they may help manage weight and reduce factors associated with metabolic syndrome.

Factors Influencing Probiotic Efficacy

1. **Fermentation Duration**: Longer fermentation times can increase the concentration of acids, which might inhibit the survival of some probiotic organisms. Finding the right balance in fermentation time is crucial to maximize the probiotic benefits.

2. **Storage Conditions**: Post-fermentation handling and storage significantly affect probiotic viability. Cold storage can help preserve these microorganisms, whereas prolonged storage at room temperature might reduce their numbers.

3. **Individual Variability**: The impact of probiotics on gut health can vary from person to person based on individual gut flora, health status, and even genetics. Not everyone will experience the same level of benefits from consuming kombucha.

Safety and Considerations

1. **Homemade vs. Commercial Kombucha**: Homemade kombucha might contain a different spectrum of bacteria and yeast compared to commercially produced varieties, which are often pasteurized or filtered to control microbial content. For those specifically seeking probiotic benefits, unpasteurized, raw kombucha is typically recommended.

2. **Potential Risks**: For people with compromised immune systems, there is a risk that some of the live bacteria and yeast in kombucha could cause infection. Such individuals should consult with a healthcare provider before adding kombucha to their diet.

The probiotic benefits of kombucha make it a valuable addition to the diet for those looking to improve digestive health, enhance immune function, and potentially support mental and metabolic health. However, the benefits can vary based on the specific attributes of the kombucha, how it is prepared, and individual health conditions. As with any dietary supplement, it is wise to consume kombucha in moderation and be aware of how your body responds to it.

Antioxidants and Detoxification

Kombucha is often lauded for its antioxidant properties and its purported detoxification benefits. Understanding the roles these factors play in health and wellness can help consumers make informed decisions about incorporating kombucha into their diets. This section explores the science behind kombucha's antioxidant content and its detoxifying effects.

Antioxidant Properties of Kombucha

1. **Sources of Antioxidants**: Kombucha's primary source of antioxidants comes from the tea used as its base, particularly green and black teas, which are rich in polyphenols such as catechins and theaflavins. These compounds are known for their

ability to scavenge free radicals, reducing oxidative stress in the body.

2. **Enhancement through Fermentation**: The fermentation process can enhance the bioavailability of these tea-derived antioxidants. As kombucha ferments, the polyphenolic compounds may be transformed into new forms that are easier for the body to use, potentially increasing their antioxidant activity.

3. **Role in Health**: Antioxidants are critical in countering oxidative stress, a factor in aging and many chronic diseases, such as cardiovascular diseases and cancers. Regular consumption of antioxidant-rich beverages like kombucha may help in maintaining overall health and reducing the risk of these conditions.

Detoxification Benefits

1. **Mechanisms of Detoxification**: Detoxification in the body involves processing and eliminating toxins through the liver, kidneys, intestines, and skin. Kombucha contains various acids, including gluconic acid and glucuronic acid, which are believed to support these processes. Glucuronic acid, in particular, is known for its role in conjugating toxins and thereby making them more water-soluble for excretion.

2. **Scientific Evidence**: While many detoxification claims are anecdotal, some studies suggest that the components in kombucha can support the liver's detoxification pathways. More research is needed to conclusively determine the extent and effectiveness of these benefits in humans.

3. **Considerations**: It's important to note that no food or beverage, including kombucha, can 'detoxify' the body in the absence of a healthy liver and kidneys. The body's detoxification systems are complex and efficiently designed to handle detoxification without

external aids. Kombucha should be seen as a supportive element rather than a cure-all.

Balancing Expectations

1. **Moderation and Variety**: While kombucha can be a valuable addition to a healthy diet due to its antioxidants, it should be consumed in moderation. A balanced diet rich in fruits, vegetables, and whole grains, along with adequate hydration, is crucial for maintaining the body's natural detoxification systems.

2. **Potential Risks**: Due to its acidity, kombucha can potentially cause digestive upset or discomfort in some individuals, particularly in those with sensitive stomachs or gastroesophageal reflux disease. As with any fermented product, homemade kombucha carries the risk of contamination if not prepared in a sanitary environment.

The antioxidants in kombucha contribute to its health benefits by potentially reducing oxidative stress, while the acids may support detoxification pathways. However, the effects are likely to be modest and should be viewed as part of a holistic approach to health. Consuming kombucha for its pleasant taste and general health benefits, rather than miraculous detox effects, is the best practice. As always, individuals should consult health professionals about their diet, especially when introducing new foods and beverages like kombucha.

Kombucha for Weight Management and Metabolic Health

Kombucha has gained attention not only for its unique flavor and probiotic benefits but also for potential roles in weight management and enhancing metabolic health. This section explores how kombucha may influence these areas, examining the underlying mechanisms and the available scientific evidence.

Kombucha and Weight Management

1. **Low-Calorie Alternative**: Kombucha is often touted as a low-calorie alternative to sugary beverages. Substituting high-calorie drinks with kombucha can help reduce overall calorie intake, which is beneficial for weight management.

2. **Effects on Appetite**: Some components in kombucha, particularly the acids and small amounts of ethanol produced during fermentation, may influence satiety and reduce appetite. However, the evidence supporting this effect is largely anecdotal, and more research is needed to confirm these potential benefits.

3. **Influence on the Gut Microbiota**: The probiotics in kombucha can help balance the gut microbiome, which is increasingly recognized as playing a significant role in weight regulation and obesity. A healthier gut microbiota may improve metabolism and fat utilization, contributing to weight control.

Kombucha and Metabolic Health

1. **Blood Sugar Control**: Kombucha's acetic acid content, similar to that in vinegar, may help to lower blood sugar levels by improving insulin sensitivity. The mechanism is thought to involve the slowing of carbohydrate digestion and an increase in the uptake of glucose by skeletal muscles, thereby reducing blood sugar spikes.

2. **Cholesterol Management**: Some studies suggest that kombucha can influence lipid metabolism, potentially lowering levels of LDL cholesterol (bad cholesterol) and increasing HDL cholesterol (good cholesterol). These effects are primarily attributed to the antioxidant properties of the tea polyphenols and their transformation during the fermentation process.

3. **Liver Health**: The liver plays a crucial role in metabolism, including the processing of fats and toxins. Kombucha's purported

detoxifying effects, mainly through compounds like glucuronic acid, may support liver function and thus enhance overall metabolic health. However, scientific studies are required to validate these claims definitively.

Scientific Evidence and Considerations

1. **Limited Research**: While there are promising indicators that kombucha may benefit weight management and metabolic health, robust scientific data are limited. Most of the current evidence comes from animal studies and in vitro experiments, which may not directly translate to effects in humans.

2. **Potential Risks**: For individuals with pre-existing health conditions, such as diabetes, it's essential to monitor kombucha consumption, particularly homemade varieties, which can vary in sugar content and acidity. Consulting with a healthcare provider before integrating kombucha into a diet for health purposes is advisable.

3. **Holistic Approach**: It's important to view kombucha as part of a broader diet and lifestyle strategy for weight and metabolic health management. Effective strategies typically involve balanced nutrition, regular physical activity, and adequate sleep.

Kombucha may offer some benefits for weight management and metabolic health, primarily through its role as a low-calorie beverage alternative with potential impacts on appetite, blood sugar control, cholesterol levels, and liver function. However, it should not be relied upon as a sole treatment for weight or metabolic issues. Continued research and a cautious, informed approach to consumption will help maximize the benefits while minimizing risks.

Addressing the Myths: What Kombucha Can and Cannot Do

Kombucha, while popular for its unique flavor and potential health benefits, is often surrounded by myths and exaggerated claims. It's important for consumers to have a clear understanding of what kombucha can realistically offer and what expectations need moderation. This section aims to demystify some of the common misconceptions about kombucha and clarify its actual benefits and limitations.

Myth 1: Kombucha is a Miracle Cure

Reality: Kombucha is not a panacea or miracle cure for diseases. While it contains several bioactive compounds such as acids, enzymes, and probiotics that may benefit health, its effects are supportive rather than curative. It should be consumed as part of a balanced diet and healthy lifestyle, not as a substitute for medical treatment.

Myth 2: Kombucha Detoxifies the Body

Reality: The liver and kidneys are the body's primary detoxification systems. While kombucha contains glucuronic acid, which is involved in detoxification processes in the liver, there is limited scientific evidence to suggest that drinking kombucha has significant detoxifying effects. The idea that it can "cleanse" the body of toxins is largely overstated.

Myth 3: Kombucha Can Help You Lose Weight Quickly

Reality: Kombucha is a low-calorie drink and can be a healthier substitute for sugary beverages, potentially helping with weight management. However, there is no evidence to suggest that kombucha alone can induce significant or rapid weight loss. Effective weight management involves a comprehensive approach including diet modifications and physical activity.

Myth 4: Kombucha Cures Digestive Issues

Reality: Kombucha contains probiotics which may help balance the gut microbiome and support digestive health. However, its effectiveness can vary widely between individuals. While some may experience improvements in digestive function, others might not see any benefit. It is also not a cure for digestive diseases and should not replace treatments prescribed by healthcare professionals.

Myth 5: Kombucha is Safe for Everyone to Drink

Reality: While kombucha is safe for most people, it contains small amounts of alcohol and caffeine, and its acidic nature may not be suitable for everyone. Individuals with gastrointestinal conditions, pregnant women, nursing mothers, and those with compromised immune systems should consult with a healthcare provider before incorporating kombucha into their diet. Additionally, homemade kombucha carries a risk of contamination if not prepared correctly.

Myth 6: All Kombucha Products Are the Same

Reality: The nutritional content and microbial composition of kombucha can vary significantly depending on the ingredients used, the fermentation process, and whether the product is pasteurized or raw. Commercially produced kombucha is often pasteurized, which can kill beneficial bacteria, whereas homemade or raw kombucha might contain more live cultures but also poses a higher risk of contamination.

Kombucha is a healthful and enjoyable beverage that can offer certain health benefits, particularly related to gut health and as a healthier alternative to sugary drinks. However, it is important to maintain realistic expectations about its capabilities and recognize that it is not a substitute for medical advice or treatment. As with any supplement or health product, consumers should do their research and consult health professionals when necessary. Enjoy kombucha for its taste and potential health benefits, but remember that it is just one part of a holistic approach to health.

Chapter 9: Troubleshooting and FAQs

Identifying and Resolving Common Issues

Brewing kombucha at home can sometimes present challenges, even for experienced brewers. Understanding how to identify and resolve common issues is crucial for maintaining the quality and safety of your kombucha. This section covers typical problems that may arise during the kombucha brewing process, along with solutions to help you quickly address and correct them.

Issue 1: Mold Growth

Symptoms: Mold on the SCOBY or in the kombucha typically appears as fuzzy, colorful spots—white, green, black, or blue. Mold growth is often due to improper sanitation, poor air circulation, or incorrect temperatures.

Solution:

- **Prevention**: Ensure all equipment is thoroughly cleaned and sanitized. Keep the brewing area well-ventilated and the kombucha covered with a breathable yet tightly woven cloth to prevent contaminants.

- **Action**: If mold appears, discard the SCOBY and the kombucha immediately. Mold cannot be safely removed or reversed, and consumption of mold-contaminated kombucha can be harmful.

Issue 2: Weak Carbonation

Symptoms: The kombucha lacks fizziness after the second fermentation.

Solution:

- **Increase Sugar Content**: Add a small amount of sugar during the bottling stage to provide more fuel for the yeast, which can boost carbonation.

- **Check Seals**: Ensure that the bottles used for second fermentation are airtight. Poor sealing can allow carbon dioxide to escape.

- **Adjust Fermentation Time**: Allow more time for the second fermentation, especially in cooler temperatures.

Issue 3: Too Sour or Vinegar-Like Flavor

Symptoms: The kombucha tastes excessively sour or like vinegar, which might happen if it's over-fermented.

Solution:

- **Shorten Fermentation Time**: Monitor the taste more frequently and shorten the first fermentation period.

- **Adjust Ratios**: Use less starter tea or a younger SCOBY to slow down the fermentation process.

- **Balance with Sweetness**: In the second fermentation, adding fruits or juices can help balance out excessive sourness.

Issue 4: Yeast Overgrowth

Symptoms: The presence of too many yeast strands can result in a strong, unpleasant yeast flavor, sediment at the bottom of the jar, or an overly alcoholic taste.

Solution:

- **Regulate Temperature**: Keep the brewing area at a moderate temperature, as high temperatures can accelerate yeast activity.

- **Remove Excess Yeast**: Before starting a new batch, rinse the SCOBY under cold water to remove excess yeast strands. Additionally, clean out the fermentation vessel thoroughly to remove any buildup.

- **Balance SCOBY**: Occasionally rotate in a new SCOBY to ensure a balanced yeast-to-bacteria ratio.

Issue 5: SCOBY Not Forming

Symptoms: A new SCOBY does not form at the top of the kombucha during fermentation, which can be due to weak starter tea, insufficient nutrients, or low temperatures.

Solution:

- **Use Strong Starter Tea**: Ensure that the starter tea is potent and acidic enough to promote SCOBY formation.

- **Optimal Temperature**: Maintain an ambient temperature within the ideal range (68-78 degrees Fahrenheit).

- **Nutrient Check**: Ensure that there's enough sugar and nutrients from the tea for the SCOBY to thrive.

Troubleshooting in kombucha brewing involves keen observation and timely adjustments. By identifying the signs of common issues early and applying the appropriate solutions, you can maintain the health of your SCOBY and the quality of your kombucha, ensuring a successful brewing experience every time.

Keeping Your SCOBY Healthy

The health of your SCOBY (Symbiotic Culture Of Bacteria and Yeast) is crucial to successful kombucha brewing. A healthy SCOBY ensures that each batch ferments properly, producing kombucha with the desired flavor and health benefits. This section provides essential guidelines for maintaining your SCOBY's health and identifying potential issues.

Understanding SCOBY Health

1. **Appearance and Texture**: A healthy SCOBY is thick, smooth, and uniform in color, ranging from white to light brown. It should feel firm and slippery, not slimy or overly mushy. The presence of brown stringy yeast particles is normal and can be gently rinsed off.

2. **Growth Patterns**: A healthy SCOBY will typically grow to cover the surface area of your brewing vessel, forming new layers with each batch. The thickness of the SCOBY can vary, but it should be robust and intact without holes or excessively thin areas.

Tips for Maintaining SCOBY Health

1. **Proper Nutrition**: Ensure your SCOBY gets adequate nutrition by using the right balance of tea and sugar. Too little sugar can starve the SCOBY, while too much can lead to an overly acidic environment that may harm it.

2. **Optimal Temperature**: Maintain a brewing temperature between 68-78 degrees Fahrenheit (20-26 degrees Celsius). Temperatures too low can slow down fermentation, causing the SCOBY to become dormant, while too high temperatures can stress the SCOBY, leading to yeast overgrowth or unwanted bacterial development.

3. **Clean Environment**: Always use clean, sanitized equipment for brewing. Contamination can introduce harmful bacteria or mold, which can damage or kill your SCOBY.

4. **Regular Refreshment**: Change out some of the older SCOBY layers and replace them with newer ones periodically. This

practice helps maintain a vigorous and healthy culture, as older SCOBYs can become less efficient over time.

Signs of SCOBY Distress

1. **Mold Growth**: Mold on a SCOBY appears fuzzy and may be green, black, white, or blue. If you see mold, discard the SCOBY and the kombucha because it is unsafe to consume.

2. **Unusual Odors**: A healthy SCOBY and kombucha should have a pleasant, slightly vinegary smell. Any rotten, cheesy, or otherwise unpleasant odors may indicate contamination or an unhealthy SCOBY.

3. **Lethargic Fermentation**: If your kombucha is not fermenting properly or the SCOBY is not forming new layers, it might not be healthy. This can occur due to inadequate temperature, poor nutrition, or an aged SCOBY.

Reviving a Weak SCOBY

1. **Rest and Recovery**: If your SCOBY seems weak, give it a rest period in fresh sweet tea in a controlled environment. Sometimes, a little break and a change of environment are all that's needed.

2. **SCOBY Hotel**: Start a SCOBY hotel where multiple SCOBYs can be stored in the same container with plenty of sweet tea. This allows weaker SCOBYs to recover and strengthen as they are not under the stress of continuous brewing.

3. **Assess and Replace**: If a SCOBY continues to perform poorly despite your best efforts, it may be time to replace it. You can obtain a new SCOBY from a healthy batch, buy one, or request one from another brewer.

Keeping your SCOBY healthy is key to producing high-quality kombucha. By providing proper nutrition, maintaining optimal environmental conditions, and regularly assessing the health of your SCOBY, you can enjoy continuous successful brewing. Remember, a healthy SCOBY is the heart of the kombucha brewing process, so give it the care and attention it deserves.

Adjusting Flavor and Carbonation

Achieving the perfect balance of flavor and carbonation in kombucha can sometimes be a challenge. This section addresses common issues related to adjusting these aspects of your brew and offers practical solutions to help you fine-tune the taste and effervescence of your kombucha.

Adjusting Flavor

1. **Too Sweet**: If your kombucha tastes too sweet, it may not have fermented long enough. Extend the fermentation period to allow more time for the sugars to be converted into acids and other compounds. This will also increase the tartness, reducing the sweet taste.

2. **Too Sour**: If the kombucha is overly sour, it has likely fermented for too long. To correct this in future batches, you can shorten the fermentation time. For the current batch, you can dilute it with sweet tea or fruit juice to balance the acidity.

3. **Flat or Bland**: Sometimes kombucha might lack depth in flavor. To enhance the flavor profile, consider adding aromatic ingredients like herbs, spices, or flavored teas during the second fermentation. Ingredients like ginger, lemon, or berries can add refreshing and complex notes.

Adjusting Carbonation

1. **Lack of Fizz**: If your kombucha isn't as fizzy as you would like, there are several potential solutions:

- **Increase Sugar During Bottling**: Adding a small amount of sugar before the second fermentation can give the yeast more to feed on, producing more carbon dioxide.

- **Secure Seal**: Ensure that the bottles are sealed tightly during the second fermentation to trap carbon dioxide and increase internal pressure, which enhances carbonation.

- **Optimal Temperature**: Carbonation typically occurs best at warmer room temperatures (around 70-80°F or 21-27°C). If your brewing environment is too cool, consider finding a warmer spot.

2. **Over Carbonation**: Overly fizzy kombucha can be problematic, leading to messy overflows upon opening. To manage this:

   - **Burp Bottles**: Periodically open the bottles during the second fermentation to release excess carbon dioxide.

   - **Shorten Second Fermentation**: Reduce the time bottles spend fermenting at room temperature before refrigeration, which slows down the fermentation and stops additional carbonation buildup.

General Tips for Flavor and Carbonation

1. **Consistent Measurements**: Use consistent measurements and timings across your batches to better control the outcomes. Keeping a brewing log can help track what works and what doesn't.

2. **Taste Regularly**: Regularly taste your kombucha during fermentation to catch and correct flavor and carbonation issues before they become too pronounced.

3. **Use Fresh Ingredients**: Fresh, high-quality ingredients not only yield better flavor but also behave more predictably during fermentation, helping you achieve the desired outcomes.

4. **Experiment in Small Batches**: When trying out new techniques or adjustments, do so in small batches. This minimizes waste if the batch doesn't turn out as expected and allows for quicker iterations to find the perfect setup.

Adjusting the flavor and carbonation of kombucha can significantly enhance its enjoyment and appeal. By understanding and controlling the factors that affect these aspects, you can produce consistently delicious and satisfying kombucha tailored to your preferences. Patience and attention to detail during experimentation are key to mastering the art of kombucha brewing.

Handling Mold and Contamination

Mold and contamination are significant concerns in kombucha brewing that can compromise the safety and quality of your brew. Understanding how to identify, prevent, and handle these issues is crucial for any kombucha brewer. This section provides detailed guidance on addressing mold growth and other forms of contamination.

Identifying Mold and Contamination

1. **Appearance of Mold**: Mold typically appears as fuzzy, colored spots on the surface of the kombucha or the SCOBY. Common colors include green, black, white, or blue. Unlike the normal yeast strands that are stringy and brownish, mold has a distinctly raised and textured appearance.

2. **Signs of Contamination**: Other signs of contamination might include off odors, sliminess, or a change in the normal color of the SCOBY. Unusual sourness or a rotten smell can also indicate bacterial contamination, which may not always be visible.

Preventing Mold and Contamination

1. **Sanitation**: Proper sanitation is the most effective way to prevent mold and contamination. All equipment, containers, and utensils

should be thoroughly cleaned and sanitized before each use. Avoid using antibacterial soap as it can leave residues that harm the SCOBY. Instead, use hot water, vinegar, or a non-rinse sanitizer designed for brewing.

2. **Proper Covering**: Ensure your brewing vessel is covered with a tight-weave cloth or coffee filter secured with a rubber band. This allows the kombucha to breathe while keeping out contaminants, including dust and insects.

3. **Correct Storage**: Store the brewing vessel in a clean, dry, and well-ventilated area away from direct sunlight and potential contaminants like trash cans or plants.

4. **Healthy SCOBY**: Always use a healthy and robust SCOBY. A weak or old SCOBY is more susceptible to mold and bacterial contamination. Refresh your SCOBY regularly and retire old or discolored ones.

Handling Mold

1. **Discard the Batch**: If you spot mold on the SCOBY or in the kombucha, the entire batch, including the SCOBY, must be discarded. Mold penetrates below the surface, and its toxins can be dangerous, making it unsafe to try to salvage the batch.

2. **Clean and Sanitize**: After discarding a contaminated batch, thoroughly clean and sanitize the brewing vessel, utensils, and any surfaces that may have come into contact with the mold. Use hot water and a vinegar solution, followed by a thorough rinse with hot water.

3. **Restart with Caution**: Obtain a new SCOBY from a reliable source before restarting your brewing process. Ensure that the new start is conducted under strictly sanitized conditions to prevent recurrence.

Handling Non-Mold Contamination

1. **Evaluate and Adjust**: If the kombucha has an off smell or taste but no visible mold, evaluate your brewing process for potential issues. This might include checking fermentation times, temperature control, and ingredient ratios.

2. **Increase Acidity**: Adjusting the pH to be more acidic can help inhibit unwanted bacterial growth. Adding a bit more starter tea to your next batch can help maintain a lower pH environment.

3. **Trial and Error**: Sometimes, non-mold issues can be resolved through trial and improvement in your brewing practices. Pay close attention to how changes in your process affect the outcome.

Mold and other forms of contamination are serious issues in kombucha brewing but can be managed with rigorous attention to cleanliness and proper brewing practices. By maintaining a clean brewing environment, using healthy SCOBYs, and being vigilant for signs of trouble, you can ensure your kombucha remains safe and enjoyable to drink.

Chapter 10: Cultural and Historical Perspectives

Kombucha's Role in Traditional Medicine

Kombucha has a storied history, particularly in traditional medicine, where it has been used for centuries across various cultures. This section explores the historical role of kombucha in traditional medicinal practices, highlighting how different cultures have utilized this fermented tea to promote health and wellness.

Origins and Early Uses

1. **Ancient China**: Often referred to as the "Tea of Immortality," kombucha is believed to have originated in Northeast China around 220 B.C. during the Tsin Dynasty. It was primarily consumed for its purported health benefits, including detoxification and energy enhancement. Ancient Chinese practitioners often recommended it to aid in digestion and to balance the body's internal energies.

2. **Spread to Russia and Eastern Europe**: By the turn of the 20th century, kombucha had made its way to Russia and from there spread to other parts of Eastern Europe. Known in Russian as "chai kvass," it was commonly used for its detoxifying and energizing properties. Traditional Eastern European medicine used kombucha to treat a wide array of conditions from simple headaches to more severe illnesses such as cancer, although scientific support for such treatments is limited.

Medicinal Claims and Beliefs

1. **Detoxification**: One of the most enduring beliefs in traditional medicine is that kombucha helps detoxify the body, particularly

the liver. This is thought to be due to the presence of glucuronic acid, which binds to toxins to facilitate their excretion.

2. **Digestive Health**: Kombucha has been traditionally used to promote digestion. The probiotics (beneficial bacteria) generated during fermentation are believed to restore balance to the gut microbiome, aiding in digestion and improving gut health.

3. **Immune Boosting**: The belief that kombucha boosts the immune system is prevalent in many cultures. This is attributed to its high antioxidant content, which helps fight free radicals, and its probiotic content, which supports the immune system.

Contemporary Understanding and Scientific Perspective

1. **Modern Evaluation**: In the contemporary health scene, kombucha is often scrutinized through scientific research to validate ancient claims. While studies have shown that kombucha contains antioxidants and probiotics, its efficacy in treating diseases traditionally claimed by folk medicine remains scientifically unproven or significantly exaggerated.

2. **Safety and Efficacy**: Modern medical practitioners often caution against the unfounded belief that kombucha can cure serious diseases. While it can be a healthy addition to a regular diet, it should not replace conventional medicine, especially for serious conditions.

3. **Holistic Use**: Today, kombucha is recommended as part of a holistic approach to health. It is valued more for its potential to support overall well-being rather than as a remedy for specific ailments.

Kombucha's role in traditional medicine spans centuries and cultures, characterized by a rich tapestry of medicinal claims. While modern science has begun to uncover the mechanisms behind some of these traditional uses, such as its probiotic and antioxidant properties, much of kombucha's historical medicinal lore remains supported more by anecdotal evidence than by rigorous scientific proof. As kombucha continues to be popular in health and wellness circles, it is important for consumers to maintain a balanced perspective on its health benefits, recognizing both its potential and its limitations.

The Socioeconomic Impact of Kombucha

Kombucha has not only been a beverage with cultural and health significance but also a product with considerable socioeconomic impacts. As kombucha has grown from a homebrewed drink to a major commercial enterprise, it has influenced economies, industries, and consumer behaviors worldwide. This section explores how kombucha has shaped and been shaped by socioeconomic factors.

Growth of the Kombucha Market

1. **Market Expansion**: Over the past few decades, the global kombucha market has seen exponential growth. Initially popular among health-conscious consumers in niche markets, kombucha has transitioned into mainstream beverage industries around the world. This growth has been driven by increasing consumer awareness of health and wellness and the rising popularity of functional beverages.

2. **Industry Impact**: The burgeoning kombucha industry has stimulated growth in related sectors, including tea production, sugar and flavoring industries, and bottle manufacturing. It has also spurred innovations in packaging and preservation technologies to extend shelf life without compromising the drink's probiotic benefits.

3. **Job Creation**: As kombucha companies have proliferated, they have created jobs across various levels of production, from brewing and fermentation to marketing, sales, and distribution.

This growth has contributed to economic development, particularly in regions where kombucha production is concentrated.

Consumer Trends and Economic Behavior

1. **Health and Wellness Trends**: The popularity of kombucha is closely tied to broader consumer trends toward natural and health-promoting products. This shift has influenced not only the beverage market but also broader consumer behavior, impacting dietary choices and lifestyle decisions.

2. **Premiumization**: As with many health-centric products, there is a trend toward premiumization in kombucha offerings. Consumers are willing to pay higher prices for kombuchas that are organic, locally sourced, or have specialized flavors or added health benefits. This trend has helped elevate kombucha to a boutique health product, influencing consumer expectations and market dynamics.

3. **DIY Culture**: The ease of kombucha brewing has also fostered a robust DIY culture, which has economic implications. Home brewing reduces reliance on commercial products and can influence local economies differently than mass-produced beverages. It also supports industries related to home brewing, such as starter kits, brewing equipment, and educational resources.

Challenges and Considerations

1. **Regulation and Standards**: As the kombucha market has grown, so has the need for regulatory oversight. Issues such as the variability in alcohol content and health claims have prompted discussions about industry standards and regulatory measures, which impact how kombucha is produced, marketed, and sold.

2. **Sustainability Concerns**: With the increase in kombucha production, sustainability has become a concern. The sourcing of ingredients, energy use, and packaging waste are all factors that influence the environmental footprint of the kombucha industry. Many producers are now looking toward more sustainable practices, which can also be a selling point to environmentally conscious consumers.

3. **Economic Volatility**: Like any trend-driven market, the kombucha industry is susceptible to economic fluctuations. Changes in consumer preferences, economic downturns, or increased competition can impact market stability.

The socioeconomic impact of kombucha extends far beyond its origins as a traditional beverage. Its rise in popularity reflects changing consumer values, impacts related industries, and stimulates economic activities in diverse ways. As kombucha continues to evolve, its ability to adapt to regulatory, environmental, and market changes will likely dictate its future trajectory in the global market.

Kombucha in Popular Culture

Kombucha has transcended its traditional roots to become a prominent feature in popular culture, particularly in Western countries. Its rise from a niche health tonic to a mainstream beverage is reflective of broader societal trends and changing consumer preferences. This section explores how kombucha has been integrated into and influenced popular culture, highlighting its impact on media, lifestyle, and consumer behavior.

Emergence in the Mainstream

1. **Health and Wellness Movement**: The proliferation of kombucha in popular culture is closely linked to the global health and wellness movement. As more people have become invested in improving their health and well-being through diet, kombucha has

been championed as a beneficial product due to its probiotic content and perceived health benefits.

2. **Celebrity Endorsements**: Kombucha has gained visibility and popularity through endorsements from celebrities who tout its health benefits. These endorsements have not only boosted its profile but have also made kombucha a fashionable beverage among health-conscious consumers.

3. **Media Exposure**: Coverage in health magazines, lifestyle blogs, and cooking shows has further elevated kombucha's status. It is often featured as a key component of detox diets and wellness routines, which has helped embed it in the popular health culture narrative.

Cultural Significance and Identity

1. **Symbol of Lifestyle**: Drinking kombucha has become associated with a modern, health-conscious lifestyle. It's often seen as a badge of health awareness and environmental responsibility, appealing particularly to millennials and Gen Z consumers who prioritize sustainability and wellness.

2. **Community and Social Identity**: Kombucha has fostered a sense of community among its enthusiasts. Homebrewing clubs, online forums, and social media groups share brewing tips, flavoring ideas, and health anecdotes, strengthening the cultural ties among kombucha drinkers.

3. **Inclusion in Social Events**: Kombucha is increasingly served at cafes, restaurants, and even bars as a non-alcoholic alternative, suitable for social events and gatherings. Its inclusion on menus further normalizes it as a mainstream beverage choice.

Impact on Consumer Markets

1. **Product Diversification**: The commercial success of kombucha has led to a diversification of products in the market. Innovations

include kombucha cocktails, kombucha-infused foods, and a variety of flavors ranging from classic fruit infusions to exotic herbal blends.

2. **Economic Influence**: As kombucha has grown in popularity, it has significantly impacted the beverage market, challenging traditional soft drinks and contributing to the rise of functional beverages. This shift has influenced investment and production strategies across the beverage industry.

3. **Retail Expansion**: Kombucha is now widely available in supermarkets, health food stores, and via direct-to-consumer platforms. This accessibility has shifted kombucha from a specialty item to a household staple.

Challenges and Controversies

1. **Health Debates**: Despite its popularity, kombucha has been at the center of health debates concerning its purported benefits, alcohol content, and safety in home brewing. These discussions have spurred research and regulatory scrutiny, shaping public perception and consumer confidence.

2. **Cultural Appropriation Concerns**: As kombucha becomes commercialized, there are growing concerns about cultural appropriation, particularly how traditional practices are adopted and adapted by different cultures without acknowledging their origins.

Kombucha's integration into popular culture is a testament to its adaptability and the shifting priorities of consumers toward healthier lifestyles. As it continues to evolve, kombucha remains a fascinating example of how traditional beverages can gain global significance and influence modern dietary trends and cultural practices.

The Ritual and Artistry of Brewing

Kombucha brewing, while often approached as a science for achieving optimal health benefits, also involves a significant measure of ritual and artistry. This aspect celebrates the cultural depth and creative expression behind kombucha making, transforming it from a mere beverage into a craft steeped in tradition and personal touch. This section explores how the ritualistic and artistic elements of kombucha brewing contribute to its cultural and personal significance.

Cultural Rituals in Kombucha Brewing

1. **Historical Roots**: The practice of brewing kombucha dates back centuries, primarily in East Asia, Russia, and Eastern Europe. Each region developed its own rituals around kombucha brewing, often tied to health, longevity, and community. In many cultures, preparing and sharing kombucha has been a way to promote wellness within families and communities, a practice that carries a sense of tradition and care.

2. **Ritualistic Elements**: The process of brewing kombucha involves several stages—brewing the tea, adding the sugar, cooling, inoculating with SCOBY, and fermenting—which can become ritualistic. Many brewers follow specific, time-honored procedures that imbue the process with personal and cultural significance. These rituals can include specific times of day for brewing, reciting prayers or thoughts for health, and even playing music to the SCOBY to influence its development.

Artistry in Flavor and Fermentation

1. **Creative Expression**: Beyond the health benefits, kombucha brewing offers an outlet for creativity, much like cooking or baking. Brewers experiment with different types of teas, sugars, and flavorings from various fruits, herbs, and spices, allowing for

endless variations and unique flavor profiles. This creative process turns each batch into a personal work of art.

2. **Aesthetic Considerations**: The presentation of kombucha can also be an artistic endeavor. The color, clarity, and carbonation are not only important for taste but also for visual appeal. The way kombucha is bottled, labeled, and served can reflect a brewer's aesthetic and cultural influences, making each bottle a representation of the brewer's artistry.

Personal and Community Engagement

1. **Sharing the Brew**: The act of sharing kombucha, whether through commercial sale or among friends and family, is a significant aspect of its culture. This practice fosters a sense of community and connection, reinforcing kombucha's role as a social beverage. In many cultures, sharing kombucha is akin to sharing a meal—a gesture of hospitality and goodwill.

2. **Educational Aspects**: Teaching others how to brew kombucha has become a popular way to engage with the community, passing on knowledge and skills that empower individuals and promote wellness. Workshops, online courses, and brewing clubs help spread the art of kombucha brewing, enriching the community's health and cultural diversity.

The ritual and artistry of kombucha brewing are what transform it from a simple beverage into a rich cultural practice. For many, kombucha is not just about drinking for health but is also an expression of creativity, a nod to tradition, and a way to connect with others. Each step in the brewing process, from selecting ingredients to sharing the final product, carries both personal and communal significance, making kombucha much more than just a fermented tea.

CHAPTER 11: BEYOND BREWING: CREATIVE USES OF KOMBUCHA

Kombucha in Mixology

Kombucha's unique profile of tartness, sweetness, and carbonation makes it an excellent ingredient in the world of mixology. Its versatility allows it to blend seamlessly into various cocktails and mocktails, providing a probiotic boost along with intriguing flavors. This section delves into the role of kombucha in cocktail creation, offering insight into its use as a mixer and the innovative drinks that can be crafted using it.

Advantages of Using Kombucha in Cocktails

1. **Flavor Complexity**: Kombucha adds a complex flavor profile that can enhance a cocktail's depth. Its natural effervescence and tartness make it an excellent substitute for traditional carbonated mixers like soda or tonic water, while the fermentation process introduces a range of subtle flavors that can complement a wide variety of spirits.

2. **Health Appeal**: Incorporating kombucha into cocktails offers a health-conscious twist, appealing to those looking to enjoy alcoholic beverages with added benefits. While the alcohol content negates some health advantages, the probiotics, enzymes, and acids in kombucha can make cocktail consumption feel less indulgent.

3. **Creativity and Innovation**: Kombucha encourages creativity in drink design. Its ability to blend with multiple types of alcohol and ingredients means that it can be used to innovate traditional recipes or create entirely new concoctions.

Popular Kombucha Cocktail Recipes

1. **Kombucha Mojito**:

   - **Ingredients**: Fresh mint leaves, lime, sugar, white rum, plain or lime-flavored kombucha, ice.

   - **Preparation**: Muddle mint, lime, and sugar in a glass. Add rum and fill the glass with ice. Top with kombucha and stir gently to combine.

2. **Kombucha Sangria**:

   - **Ingredients**: A bottle of red or white wine, seasonal fruits (like oranges, lemons, apples, and berries), a splash of brandy (optional), berry or citrus kombucha.

   - **Preparation**: In a large pitcher, combine chopped fruits, wine, and brandy. Refrigerate for at least 4 hours. Before serving, add kombucha and stir gently to mix.

3. **Kombucha Margarita**:

   - **Ingredients**: Tequila, triple sec, lime juice, agave syrup, plain or ginger kombucha, salt for rimming, lime wedge for garnish.

   - **Preparation**: Rim a glass with lime and dip in salt. Mix tequila, triple sec, lime juice, and agave syrup in a shaker with ice. Shake well and strain into the glass. Top with kombucha and garnish with a lime wedge.

Tips for Using Kombucha in Mixology

1. **Choose Complementary Flavors**: Select kombucha flavors that complement the spirit and other ingredients in your cocktail. For example, a ginger-lemon kombucha works well with whiskey, while a berry kombucha pairs nicely with vodka.

2. **Consider Sweetness Levels**: Kombucha varies in sweetness depending on its fermentation stage. Adjust the other sweet components of your cocktail accordingly to maintain balance.

3. **Temperature Considerations**: Kombucha is best used cold to preserve its probiotic content and carbonation. Add it last to cocktails to keep it refreshing and bubbly.

Kombucha's integration into mixology not only broadens the horizon of cocktail crafting but also introduces a healthier twist to enjoying mixed drinks. Whether used in a casual home setting or a professional bar, kombucha can transform traditional cocktails into innovative, health-conscious beverages that cater to modern tastes and dietary preferences. As kombucha continues to grow in popularity, its role in mixology is set to expand, paving the way for more creative and health-focused beverage options.

Crafting Vinegars and Other Byproducts

Kombucha's versatility extends beyond its traditional use as a beverage. When further fermented, it can transform into a rich vinegar or be used to create various other byproducts. This section explores how to craft kombucha vinegar and other derivatives, offering guidance on how to utilize every part of the kombucha brewing process.

Kombucha Vinegar

1. **Extended Fermentation**: To make kombucha vinegar, extend the fermentation process beyond the usual period required for drinking kombucha. Allow the kombucha to ferment for several weeks until it reaches a high level of acidity and the sweetness is almost entirely gone. This extended fermentation not only increases the acetic acid content, mimicking the qualities of traditional vinegars but also develops a more complex flavor profile.

2. **Uses of Kombucha Vinegar**: Kombucha vinegar can be used similarly to apple cider vinegar or other mild vinegars. It's excellent for salad dressings, marinades, and as a digestive tonic. Kombucha vinegar can also be used for household cleaning, as a hair rinse, or for skincare, offering a natural alternative to chemical products.

3. **Production Tips**: To ensure a consistent and safe product, keep the brewing vessel in a warm, dark place and cover it with a breathable cloth to prevent contaminants while allowing the liquid to breathe. Test the pH regularly to ensure it has reached vinegar acidity levels (typically a pH of 2-3).

SCOBY Byproducts

1. **SCOBY Snacks and Jerky**: The SCOBY itself can be repurposed into edible products. Thinly slice the SCOBY, marinate it in a mixture of spices and sauces, and dehydrate the slices to make SCOBY jerky or fruit leather-like snacks. These are not only nutritious but also a great way to reduce waste.

2. **SCOBY Dog Treats**: For pet lovers, SCOBY can be used to make probiotic-rich treats for dogs. Dehydrate small pieces of SCOBY without any additives or spices, and offer them to your pet as a healthy treat.

3. **Composting**: If you have excess SCOBY that you cannot use, consider adding it to your compost pile. SCOBY is biodegradable and can enrich your compost with bacteria and yeast that benefit soil health.

Creative Uses in Crafts

1. **Biofabrication**: On a more experimental note, SCOBY can be used in the field of biofabrication to create sustainable materials that resemble leather. This 'SCOBY leather' can be grown to

desired thicknesses, dried, and then used to craft various items such as wallets, belts, and other accessories.

2. **Art Projects**: SCOBY's unique texture and form make it an interesting medium for artistic projects. It can be dyed, shaped, and molded into various decorative items, showcasing the intersection of science and art.

The potential uses of kombucha and its byproducts are vast and varied. From creating flavorful vinegars to repurposing the SCOBY into snacks, crafts, or even sustainable fabrics, kombucha offers more than just a health drink. By exploring these creative uses, brewers can expand their kombucha practices to include a wide range of sustainable and innovative products, fully embracing the versatility of this fascinating ferment.

Beauty and Health Applications

Kombucha, renowned for its health benefits when consumed, also holds promise in beauty and topical health applications. This versatile ferment can be utilized in various ways to enhance skin health and beauty routines. This section explores how to incorporate kombucha into your beauty regimen, highlighting its potential benefits and offering practical advice for use.

Kombucha as a Skin Care Ingredient

1. **Antioxidant Properties**: Kombucha is rich in antioxidants, which help combat free radicals that can cause premature aging of the skin. Using kombucha in skin care routines can help maintain healthy, vibrant skin.

2. **Acidic Nature**: The naturally occurring acids in kombucha, such as gluconic acid, can gently exfoliate and improve skin texture. Its mild acidity helps to restore the skin's natural pH balance, enhancing the skin's protective barrier.

3. **Probiotic Benefits**: The microbial content of kombucha may also benefit the skin microbiome, promoting healthier skin that is less prone to issues like acne and eczema.

Creating Kombucha Skin Care Products

1. **Kombucha Toner**: Use kombucha as a facial toner by applying it with a cotton pad after cleansing. Its astringent properties can help tighten the pores and refresh the skin. For added benefits, infuse the kombucha with herbs like chamomile or lavender before use.

2. **Kombucha Face Masks**: Mix kombucha with natural ingredients like honey, clay, or oatmeal to create nourishing face masks. Apply the mask to clean skin, leave it on for 10-15 minutes, then rinse with warm water. This can help hydrate and rejuvenate the skin.

3. **Kombucha in Lotions and Serums**: For those who make homemade lotions or serums, adding a small amount of kombucha can introduce probiotic and antioxidant properties to the formulations, enhancing their skin health benefits.

Health Applications

1. **Scalp Treatments**: Kombucha can be used as a scalp tonic due to its probiotic and acidic properties, which may help balance scalp pH and control issues like dandruff. Simply massage diluted kombucha into the scalp before shampooing.

2. **Wound Healing**: The acidic nature of kombucha may help with minor cuts or skin irritations. It can act as a disinfectant, and the biofilm (SCOBY) can be used as a natural bandage to cover wounds, although this should be approached with caution and proper medical advice.

Safety and Sensitivity Considerations

1. **Patch Test**: Always perform a patch test before applying kombucha or any new product extensively, especially on sensitive skin. Apply a small amount to a discreet area and wait 24-48 hours to check for adverse reactions.

2. **Dilution**: Pure kombucha may be too acidic for direct application to the skin. Dilute it with water or blend it with other soothing ingredients to mitigate its potency and reduce the risk of irritation.

3. **Sun Sensitivity**: Products containing acids can make the skin more sensitive to the sun. Use sun protection and limit sun exposure when using kombucha-based skin treatments.

Incorporating kombucha into beauty and health routines is an innovative way to extend the benefits of this fermented tea beyond dietary consumption. Its natural acids, antioxidants, and probiotics offer various potential benefits for skin and hair care. However, as with any topical application, it is essential to consider individual skin sensitivity and to use such products thoughtfully to ensure safety and effectiveness.

Kombucha as a Plant Fertilizer

Kombucha, widely celebrated for its health benefits for humans, can also be a valuable addition to plant care routines. The nutrients and microbial content in kombucha make it an excellent natural fertilizer, promoting plant health and growth. This section explores how to use kombucha in gardening and plant care, discussing its benefits and methods of application.

Benefits of Kombucha for Plants

1. **Nutrient-Rich**: Kombucha contains a variety of nutrients that are beneficial to plants, including nitrogen, phosphorus, and potassium, along with a range of micronutrients that can enhance plant growth and soil health.

2. **Microbial Content**: The microbial cultures in kombucha, including beneficial bacteria and yeasts, can contribute to the soil's microbial diversity. These microbes can help break down organic material in the soil, making nutrients more available to plants and potentially improving soil structure.

3. **pH Modulation**: The slight acidity of kombucha can help modulate soil pH levels, which can be beneficial for plants that thrive in slightly acidic soils. However, it's important to monitor soil pH regularly to ensure it remains within an optimal range for your specific plants.

How to Use Kombucha as Fertilizer

1. **Dilution Is Key**: Pure kombucha is too acidic and concentrated to use directly on plants and can cause harm if not properly diluted. A safe ratio is typically 1 part kombucha to 10 parts water. This dilution helps spread the benefits of kombucha while minimizing the risk of acid burn to plant roots.

2. **Application Methods**:

   - **Soil Drench**: Use the diluted kombucha mixture to water plants, applying it directly to the soil. This method helps deliver nutrients and beneficial microbes directly to the plant's root system, where they can be most effective.

   - **Foliar Spray**: Kombucha can also be applied as a foliar spray after additional dilution (1 part kombucha to 20 parts water). Spraying the leaves can help in nutrient absorption through the stomata and may provide direct microbial benefits to the plant's surface.

3. **Frequency of Use**: Kombucha fertilizer should be used sparingly as part of a balanced plant care routine. Start by applying once every 4-6 weeks and observe how your plants respond. Adjust frequency based on plant health and growth patterns.

Precautions and Considerations

1. **Monitor Plant Response**: Always keep an eye on how plants respond after applying kombucha. Signs of distress may include yellowing leaves, drooping, or burned tips, which could indicate over-application or too strong a concentration.

2. **Use Fresh Kombucha**: For the best results, use fresh kombucha that hasn't been flavored or carbonated. Flavored kombuchas might contain sugars and additives that can attract pests or cause mold growth.

3. **Complement with Other Practices**: While kombucha can be a beneficial addition to your gardening routine, it should not replace other essential practices such as regular watering, proper fertilization, and pest management. Kombucha works best as a complement to a holistic care approach.

Using kombucha as a plant fertilizer is an innovative way to recycle this probiotic-rich beverage and extend its benefits to the garden. With proper application, kombucha can help nourish plants, enrich the soil, and support sustainable gardening practices. As with any new treatment, starting with cautious experimentation and adjusting based on specific plant needs and responses will yield the best results.

Chapter 12: Building and Nurturing a Kombucha Community

Case Studies: Stories from Around the World

Kombucha has a rich and varied history that spans many cultures and continents. As its popularity grows, so too does the community of brewers and enthusiasts who share their unique stories and experiences. This section explores several case studies from around the world, highlighting how kombucha has influenced communities, sparked business ventures, and inspired sustainable practices.

Case Study 1: The Kombucha Cooperative in Berlin, Germany

Background: In Berlin, a city known for its vibrant alternative and health-conscious communities, a group of kombucha enthusiasts founded a cooperative brewery in 2018. This cooperative focuses not only on brewing kombucha but also on promoting sustainability and community health.

Impact: The cooperative uses locally sourced, organic ingredients and operates with zero-waste principles. It has become a hub for educational workshops on fermentation and sustainable living, strengthening community ties and promoting healthier lifestyles.

Outcome: The success of the Berlin Kombucha Cooperative has inspired similar initiatives in other European cities, showcasing the potential of kombucha to foster community engagement and environmental consciousness.

Case Study 2: Kombucha Microenterprise in Nairobi, Kenya

Background: In Nairobi, a local entrepreneur started a small-scale kombucha business in 2015 to address both health issues and unemployment in her community. Using traditional African teas and local ingredients, her kombucha quickly gained popularity.

Impact: The business provides jobs and training in kombucha brewing and business skills to local youth, particularly women. The kombucha produced is marketed as a healthy, affordable alternative to sugary sodas.

Outcome: The enterprise has not only improved the economic prospects of many individuals but also raised awareness about healthy consumption practices, contributing to the community's overall well-being.

Case Study 3: Community Healing with Kombucha in Fukushima, Japan

Background: After the 2011 earthquake and nuclear disaster, residents of Fukushima faced immense health and environmental challenges. A local doctor began promoting kombucha as a way to support community health and remove toxins from the body.

Impact: The project started with teaching locals to brew kombucha at home, using it as a daily health supplement. The community embraced this practice, which helped not only in health improvement but also in bringing people together for a common cause during recovery.

Outcome: Kombucha brewing has become part of the local culture in Fukushima, symbolizing resilience and the power of community-based approaches to health and healing.

Case Study 4: Artisan Kombucha Movement in Portland, Oregon, USA

Background: Known for its artisanal food scene, Portland became a hotspot for kombucha creativity in the early 2010s. Local brewers experimented with a variety of unconventional flavors and fermentation techniques, setting new trends in the kombucha market.

Impact: This innovation led to a proliferation of small businesses and a wide range of kombucha products, making Portland a global leader in kombucha brewing and experimentation.

Outcome: The Portland kombucha scene has helped elevate the profile of kombucha from a niche health drink to a mainstream beverage, influencing global markets and consumer preferences.

These case studies illustrate the diverse ways in which kombucha can play a role in community building, economic development, and health promotion. Each story is a testament to the adaptability of kombucha brewing and its potential to bring people together across different cultures and backgrounds. The global kombucha community continues to grow, driven by shared values of health, sustainability, and innovation.

Forming Local and Online Kombucha Groups

Kombucha enthusiasts often seek community to share experiences, knowledge, and innovations. Forming local and online kombucha groups can enhance this communal spirit, providing platforms for support, learning, and sharing. This section outlines strategies for establishing and nurturing both local and online kombucha communities.

Establishing Local Kombucha Groups

1. **Initial Meetups**: Start by organizing informal meetups through social media platforms like Facebook or community bulletin boards. Local health food stores, cafes, or community centers can serve as meetup venues. These gatherings can be used to share

brewing techniques, taste different kombucha brews, and discuss health benefits.

2. **Workshops and Demonstrations**: Organize workshops where experienced brewers demonstrate various brewing methods, flavoring techniques, and discuss SCOBY care. This hands-on approach helps new brewers learn directly through experience and encourages more seasoned brewers to share their expertise.

3. **Local Kombucha Fairs and Tastings**: Host kombucha tasting events or fairs where local brewers can showcase their unique brews. This not only fosters community engagement but also helps to popularize kombucha within the broader community.

4. **Community Brewing Projects**: Initiate community brewing projects or cooperative brewing facilities where members can come together to brew, sharing resources and knowledge. This can be particularly appealing in urban areas where individuals may lack the space to brew at home.

Building Online Kombucha Communities

1. **Social Media Platforms**: Utilize platforms like Facebook, Instagram, and Reddit to create groups or pages dedicated to kombucha brewing. These platforms allow members from around the world to connect, share advice, and provide support.

2. **Webinars and Live Streams**: Conduct regular webinars and live streaming sessions with kombucha experts who can answer questions in real-time and provide updates on the latest trends and research in kombucha brewing.

3. **Online Workshops and Courses**: Develop or collaborate on online courses that teach kombucha brewing techniques from beginner to advanced levels. These can include video tutorials, downloadable resources, and forums for discussion.

4. **Virtual Tasting Sessions**: Organize virtual kombucha tastings where participants brew their own kombucha and then share their experiences and feedback during a video call. This can replicate the communal aspect of local tastings in a digital format.

Enhancing Community Engagement

1. **Regular Communication**: Maintain regular communication with community members through newsletters, social media updates, and regular meetings or webinars. Consistent engagement helps keep the community active and informed.

2. **Inclusive Environment**: Encourage a welcoming and inclusive environment where all members, regardless of their kombucha brewing expertise, feel valued and able to contribute. Emphasize learning and curiosity over competition.

3. **Feedback and Adaptation**: Regularly solicit feedback from community members on what they find valuable or would like to see changed. This feedback loop can help the community evolve to better meet the needs of its members.

Creating local and online kombucha groups provides valuable opportunities for enthusiasts to connect, learn, and share their passion for kombucha brewing. These communities not only spread knowledge and foster friendships but also contribute to the wider acceptance and understanding of kombucha as a healthful and enjoyable beverage. As these groups grow, they continually enrich the kombucha culture, blending tradition with innovative practices for brewers everywhere.

Organizing Workshops and Events

Organizing workshops and events is an effective way to build and nurture a kombucha community. These gatherings can educate, engage, and connect enthusiasts of all levels, from beginners to experienced brewers. This section provides a detailed guide on how to organize successful kombucha-related workshops and events, ensuring they are educational, enjoyable, and enriching for all participants.

Planning Your Workshop or Event

1. **Define Objectives**: Start by defining what you want to achieve with your event. Are you aiming to educate newcomers, explore advanced brewing techniques, or simply provide a space for enthusiasts to connect and share their brews? Clear objectives will guide all other aspects of your planning.

2. **Choose the Format**: Decide whether the event will be a hands-on workshop, a lecture, a tasting session, or a combination of these. The format should align with your objectives and be suitable for your target audience.

3. **Select a Venue**: Choose a venue that supports your event's format. Local community centers, co-working spaces, or local breweries can be ideal choices. Ensure the venue has the necessary facilities, such as a kitchen or large tables for brewing demonstrations and enough seating for all participants.

4. **Schedule the Event**: Pick a date and time that is likely to be convenient for most people. Consider holding events on weekends or evenings when more people are available.

5. **Prepare Materials and Equipment**: Depending on the event type, you may need brewing kits, sample kombucha, ingredients for flavor experiments, projectors for presentations, and handouts or digital resources for attendees.

Promoting Your Workshop or Event

1. **Use Social Media**: Leverage social media platforms to promote your event. Create engaging posts and updates that highlight the benefits of attending your workshop or event. Use appropriate

hashtags, and consider paid ads if you want to reach a broader audience.

2. **Engage Local Community Groups**: Reach out to local health food stores, yoga studios, and cafes that might be willing to promote your event. They can place flyers and even talk to their customers about the upcoming event.

3. **Offer Incentives**: Early bird discounts, group discounts, or offers to bring a friend for a reduced price can increase early sign-ups and larger attendance.

Conducting the Workshop or Event

1. **Registration and Welcome**: Make registration a smooth process. Provide a warm welcome to create a friendly atmosphere that encourages interaction among participants.

2. **Deliver Content**: Whether you're teaching brewing techniques, discussing the health benefits of kombucha, or leading a tasting session, ensure your content is well-organized and engaging. Use visual aids, handouts, and real-life examples to enrich the learning experience.

3. **Interactive Elements**: Include interactive segments such as Q&A sessions, group discussions, or hands-on brewing. These elements make workshops more engaging and memorable for participants.

4. **Feedback Collection**: At the end of the event, collect feedback to understand what participants liked and what could be improved. This information is invaluable for planning future events.

After the Event

1. **Follow-Up**: Send a thank you message to attendees, providing additional resources, answering any follow-up questions, and possibly a discount or early notification about future events.

2. **Share Highlights**: Post highlights from the event on social media or your community platform. This not only shows the success of your event but also engages those who could not attend.

3. **Plan the Next Steps**: Based on the feedback and your observations, start planning your next workshop or event. Continual improvement will help grow your community and keep members engaged.

Workshops and events are powerful tools for building a vibrant kombucha community. They provide a platform for education, sharing, and connection, helping to spread the passion for kombucha brewing to a wider audience. With careful planning, effective promotion, and engaging delivery, your kombucha workshops and events can become key highlights within the community calendar.

The Role of Social Media

Social media is a pivotal tool in building and nurturing a kombucha community. It offers a platform to share knowledge, connect with fellow enthusiasts, and promote kombucha-related activities. This section outlines how to effectively use social media to engage with and expand your kombucha community, fostering a vibrant and interactive environment.

Establishing a Social Media Presence

1. **Choose the Right Platforms**: Depending on your target audience, select platforms that best cater to your demographic. Instagram and Facebook are ideal for sharing images and longer posts, while Twitter can be great for quick updates and engaging in broader conversations. YouTube or TikTok can be used for video tutorials and creative kombucha content.

2. **Create Engaging Content**: Share a variety of content such as brewing tips, health benefits, flavor ideas, and behind-the-scenes

looks at kombucha brewing processes. High-quality photos, insightful posts, and engaging videos can attract followers and encourage interaction.

3. **Consistency is Key**: Regular posting is crucial to keep your audience engaged. Create a content calendar to plan your posts in advance. This helps maintain a consistent presence and ensures a mix of content types.

Leveraging Social Media for Community Engagement

1. **Interactive Posts**: Encourage interaction through questions, polls, or contests. For example, ask your followers to share their favorite flavor combinations or their kombucha brewing experiences. This not only boosts engagement but also makes your followers feel like part of a community.

2. **Live Sessions**: Host live brewing sessions, Q&A panels, or discussions on topics of interest. Live interactions can build a stronger connection with your audience and provide real-time engagement.

3. **User-Generated Content**: Encourage your community members to share their own kombucha photos and stories. Reposting user-generated content not only provides authentic testimonials but also fosters a sense of belonging and appreciation among community members.

Promoting Events and Workshops

1. **Event Announcements**: Use social media to promote upcoming workshops, meetups, or online webinars. Detailed posts with time, date, location, and what to expect can help boost attendance.

2. **Event Reminders**: Regular reminders leading up to the event can keep the date on your audience's radar and increase turnout. Include countdowns or "last chance to register" posts to create urgency.

3. **Live Coverage**: During events, share live updates or stream parts of the event to engage those who couldn't attend in person. This can broaden your reach and may increase interest in future events.

Building Brand Partnerships

1. **Collaborate with Influencers**: Partner with social media influencers who share an interest in health, wellness, or fermentation. Their endorsement can introduce your kombucha community to a broader audience.

2. **Partner with Local Businesses**: Engage with local health food stores, cafes, and markets to cross-promote content. This can help reach a local audience and build stronger community ties.

Monitoring and Analytics

1. **Track Engagement**: Use social media analytics tools to monitor which types of content perform best. Analyzing engagement rates, follower growth, and interaction patterns can help refine your strategy and content.

2. **Feedback and Adaptation**: Pay attention to comments and direct messages to gauge the community's needs and preferences. This feedback is valuable for adjusting your approach and content to better serve your community.

Social media is an essential component in the modern toolkit for building and nurturing a kombucha community. It provides a dynamic platform for education, engagement, and growth. By strategically using social media, you can create a thriving community of kombucha enthusiasts who are informed, connected, and actively involved.

CHAPTER 13: THE BUSINESS OF KOMBUCHA

Navigating Legal Requirements

Starting a kombucha business involves more than just perfecting your brew; it also requires navigating various legal requirements to ensure compliance and protect your business. This section outlines the essential legal considerations any kombucha entrepreneur should address.

Business Registration and Licensing

1. **Business Structure**: Decide on the legal structure of your business, whether it be a sole proprietorship, partnership, LLC (Limited Liability Company), or corporation. Each has different implications for liability, taxation, and ongoing requirements.

2. **Business License**: Obtain a business license from your local city or county. The process and fees vary depending on your location and the size of your operation.

3. **Health Department Permits**: Since kombucha is a consumable product, you'll need to comply with health department regulations, which may involve kitchen inspections and specific sanitary requirements. You might also need a food handler's permit, depending on your role in the production process.

Complying with Food Safety Regulations

1. **FDA Regulations**: In the United States, kombucha is regulated by the Food and Drug Administration (FDA) as a food product. You must comply with the FDA's guidelines for food safety,

which include proper labeling, facility inspections, and product testing.

2. **State and Local Regulations**: Check for any additional state and local regulations that may apply to your kombucha brewing and sales. This can include specific health code regulations that are not covered by FDA rules.

3. **Hazard Analysis and Critical Control Points (HACCP) Plan**: Developing an HACCP plan can be essential, particularly if you plan to scale your operations. This plan helps identify critical points in the brewing process where contamination or other safety issues could occur and outlines how to control these risks.

Alcohol Compliance

1. **Alcohol Content Testing**: Kombucha naturally contains trace amounts of alcohol due to fermentation. Regularly test your kombucha to ensure that the alcohol content stays below the legal threshold (typically 0.5% alcohol by volume) for non-alcoholic beverages.

2. **TTB Regulations**: If your kombucha consistently tests above the legal alcohol limit, you may need to comply with the Alcohol and Tobacco Tax and Trade Bureau (TTB) regulations, which include obtaining a brewer's permit, paying alcohol taxes, and adhering to labeling requirements.

Labeling and Marketing

1. **Accurate Labeling**: Ensure your labels accurately reflect the contents of your kombucha. Key information includes ingredients, nutrition facts, potential allergens, net contents, and the name and address of the manufacturer or distributor.

2. **Health Claims**: Be cautious about making health claims on your labels or in marketing materials. Claims must be substantiated by

scientific evidence and comply with FDA guidelines to avoid misleading consumers.

Intellectual Property Protection

1. **Trademark**: Consider trademarking your brand name, logo, and unique product names to protect your brand identity and prevent others from using similar marks.

2. **Trade Secrets**: Keep proprietary brewing methods and recipes confidential to maintain a competitive edge. Implement non-disclosure agreements (NDAs) with employees and partners as needed.

Insurance

1. **General Liability Insurance**: This type of insurance protects against potential legal hazards, such as customer injuries (e.g., from a broken bottle) or illnesses claimed to be caused by your product.

2. **Product Liability Insurance**: Essential for any food product manufacturer, this insurance covers you if your kombucha is found to be faulty or harmful after distribution.

Navigating the legal landscape is crucial for establishing and maintaining a successful kombucha business. Compliance with local, state, and federal regulations not only protects your business from legal issues but also builds trust with your customers. It's advisable to consult with legal and food industry experts to ensure that all your bases are covered as you grow your kombucha business.

Steps to Launching a Kombucha Business

Starting a kombucha business involves several key steps, from conceptualization to the actual launch. This section provides a structured roadmap for entrepreneurs looking to enter the kombucha market, detailing each critical phase in the process.

Step 1: Market Research

1. **Understand Your Audience**: Identify your target market. Are they health-conscious consumers, millennials, or perhaps local businesses like cafes and health food stores? Understanding your audience will guide your product development, branding, and marketing strategies.

2. **Analyze Competitors**: Study existing kombucha brands in your target market. What are they offering, and what can you do differently or better? Assess their pricing, flavors, packaging, and distribution channels.

3. **Regulatory Requirements**: Research the legal and health regulations related to kombucha production in your area. This includes FDA guidelines, local health codes, and any requirements for alcoholic content monitoring.

Step 2: Business Planning

1. **Business Model**: Decide on a business model. Will you focus on direct consumer sales, wholesale, online distribution, or a combination of these channels?

2. **Financial Planning**: Prepare detailed financial projections including startup costs, ongoing expenses, and revenue forecasts. Consider the costs of ingredients, equipment, packaging, labor, marketing, and distribution.

3. **Funding**: Identify sources of funding. Options might include personal savings, small business loans, investor funding, or crowdfunding.

Step 3: Product Development

1. **Recipe Formulation**: Develop and refine your kombucha recipes. Consider creating a range of flavors to appeal to different taste

preferences. Ensure your product consistently meets safety standards regarding pH and alcohol content.

2. **Branding and Packaging**: Develop a strong brand identity that resonates with your target market. Design packaging that not only looks appealing but also preserves the quality of the kombucha through proper sealing and materials.

Step 4: Setup Production

1. **Production Facility**: Set up a brewing facility that complies with local health and safety regulations. This might involve renting a commercial kitchen or setting up a designated brewing space that meets all regulatory requirements.

2. **Supplies and Equipment**: Acquire all necessary brewing equipment and ingredients. This includes brewing vessels, fermentation tanks, pH meters, thermometers, filters, bottles, labels, and raw materials like tea, sugar, and flavorings.

3. **Quality Control**: Implement quality control measures to ensure each batch of kombucha is of high quality and consistency. This includes regular pH and alcohol testing during and after fermentation.

Step 5: Marketing and Sales

1. **Marketing Strategy**: Develop a marketing plan that includes online and offline marketing tactics. Utilize social media, local events, tastings, and partnerships to build brand awareness.

2. **Distribution Channels**: Establish distribution channels. This could be direct-to-consumer through farmers' markets and online sales, or through local grocery stores, cafes, and restaurants.

3. **Launch Strategy**: Plan a launch event or promotion to generate interest and drive initial sales. Consider offering free samples, limited-time discounts, or bundled deals.

Step 6: Launch and Scale

1. **Official Launch**: Launch your business with a strong marketing push. Ensure that your production can meet the anticipated demand.

2. **Customer Feedback**: Gather and analyze customer feedback to refine your products and services continually.

3. **Scaling Up**: As your business grows, consider scaling up production, expanding product lines, or entering new markets.

Launching a kombucha business requires careful planning and execution, with attention to product quality, compliance with health regulations, and effective marketing. By following these steps, entrepreneurs can establish a solid foundation for a successful kombucha brand that resonates with consumers and stands out in the competitive marketplace.

Marketing Strategies for Small Kombucha Businesses

Marketing is crucial for small kombucha businesses looking to establish a foothold in a competitive market. Effective marketing strategies can help increase visibility, attract customers, and build a loyal following. This section outlines key marketing tactics tailored for small kombucha businesses aiming to make a significant impact.

Understanding Your Unique Selling Proposition (USP)

1. **Identify Your USP**: Determine what makes your kombucha unique. Is it your exotic flavor combinations, local sourcing, organic ingredients, health benefits, or environmentally friendly packaging? Understanding and articulating your USP is critical in differentiating your brand from competitors.

2. **Communicate Your USP**: Once identified, ensure your USP is clearly communicated in all marketing materials, from your website to social media, and on your product labels.

Building an Online Presence

1. **Website**: Create a professional website that reflects your brand's identity. Include sections about your products, brewing process, and the story behind your business. Ensure the website is SEO-optimized to improve visibility on search engines.

2. **Social Media**: Leverage platforms like Instagram, Facebook, and Twitter to connect with your audience. Use these platforms to share engaging content such as behind-the-scenes photos, customer testimonials, health tips, and product news. Regularly engage with your followers through comments and messages.

3. **Content Marketing**: Develop a content marketing strategy that could include blogging about kombucha health benefits, recipes, and brewing techniques. Share these posts on your social media channels to drive traffic to your website.

Utilizing Local Markets and Community Engagement

1. **Local Markets and Events**: Participate in local farmers' markets, health expos, and food festivals to increase brand exposure. These venues are ideal for product sampling and direct interaction with potential customers.

2. **Partnerships with Local Businesses**: Partner with local cafes, health food stores, and restaurants to carry your kombucha. Collaborations with local fitness centers and yoga studios can also help reach your target audience.

3. **Community Projects**: Engage in community projects or sponsor local events to build brand goodwill and recognition. This not only increases visibility but also establishes your brand as a responsible community member.

Leveraging Customer Feedback and Loyalty Programs

1. **Collect Customer Feedback**: Encourage customers to provide feedback through online reviews, social media, or direct surveys. Use this feedback to improve your products and customer service.

2. **Loyalty Programs**: Create a loyalty program that rewards repeat customers with discounts, special offers, or exclusive content. This can enhance customer retention and encourage word-of-mouth promotion.

Creative and Targeted Advertising

1. **Digital Advertising**: Use digital advertising platforms like Google Ads and Facebook Ads to reach a targeted audience. Tailor your ads based on demographics, interests, and behavior to maximize conversion rates.

2. **Influencer Marketing**: Collaborate with influencers who align with your brand's values and have an engaged following in the health and wellness space. This can effectively reach a larger audience and lend credibility to your product.

3. **Email Marketing**: Build an email list from your website and at events. Use this list to send out newsletters, promotions, and updates about your kombucha business. Personalize your emails to increase engagement.

Effective marketing is vital for the growth and sustainability of small kombucha businesses. By leveraging a combination of online presence, community engagement, customer feedback, and targeted advertising, you can build a strong brand that attracts and retains loyal customers. Tailor these strategies to match your resources and business goals, and be prepared to adapt to changing market conditions and customer preferences.

Sustainability in Kombucha Production

Sustainability is becoming increasingly important in the food and beverage industry, and kombucha production is no exception. As a business committed to health and wellness, implementing sustainable practices not only supports the environment but also aligns with the values of health-conscious consumers. This section explores strategies for enhancing sustainability in kombucha production, from sourcing to packaging and waste management.

Sustainable Sourcing

1. **Organic Ingredients**: Opt for organic tea, sugar, and flavorings to minimize your environmental impact. Organic farming eliminates the use of synthetic pesticides and fertilizers, which are harmful to ecosystems.

2. **Local Suppliers**: Source ingredients locally when possible to reduce carbon footprint associated with transportation. Supporting local suppliers also helps boost the local economy and ensures fresher ingredients.

3. **Fair Trade Certification**: When sourcing ingredients from overseas, consider suppliers with Fair Trade certifications. This ensures that products are economically sustainable and ethically sourced, supporting fair labor practices and community development.

Energy Efficiency in Brewing

1. **Energy-Efficient Equipment**: Invest in energy-efficient brewing and fermentation equipment to reduce electricity consumption. This includes high-efficiency heaters and cooling systems.

2. **Renewable Energy Sources**: Consider using renewable energy sources such as solar or wind power for your production facility. This reduces reliance on fossil fuels and decreases greenhouse gas emissions.

3. **Process Optimization**: Regularly review and optimize your brewing processes to reduce energy and water consumption. For example, recapturing heat from pasteurization processes to use in pre-heating can significantly reduce energy usage.

Waste Management

1. **Recycling Waste**: Implement a comprehensive recycling program for all recyclable waste in your production facility, including glass, plastic, and cardboard.

2. **Composting**: SCOBYs and other organic waste products from kombucha production are compostable. Setting up a composting system can turn waste into valuable compost for local farming or gardening projects.

3. **Water Conservation**: Implement systems to reduce water usage, such as recirculating cleaning systems for washing equipment. Additionally, treat and reuse wastewater whenever possible, adhering to local regulations regarding wastewater treatment.

Sustainable Packaging

1. **Eco-Friendly Packaging**: Choose packaging materials that are recyclable, biodegradable, or made from post-consumer recycled content. Glass bottles, while heavier than plastic, can be reused and recycled indefinitely. If using plastic, opt for types that are easily recycled.

2. **Bulk Offerings**: Provide options for customers to purchase kombucha in bulk to reduce packaging waste. This could include larger containers or encouraging customers to bring their own containers for refills.

3. **Minimalist Design**: Reduce the use of unnecessary packaging components such as plastic labels or shrink wraps. Opt for labels made with eco-friendly inks and materials.

Educating Consumers and Stakeholders

1. **Consumer Awareness**: Educate your customers about the sustainable aspects of your production process. Highlight the benefits of supporting sustainable practices in the products they choose to purchase.

2. **Engage with Stakeholders**: Work closely with suppliers, distributors, and retailers to encourage more widespread adoption of sustainable practices. Sharing knowledge and resources can help improve the sustainability of the entire supply chain.

Implementing sustainable practices in kombucha production not only minimizes environmental impact but also resonates with eco-conscious consumers, enhancing brand loyalty and market competitiveness. By focusing on sustainable sourcing, energy efficiency, waste management, and eco-friendly packaging, kombucha producers can lead by example in the movement towards a more sustainable future.

CHAPTER 14: LOOKING AHEAD: THE FUTURE OF KOMBUCHA

Innovations in Kombucha Brewing

As kombucha continues to grow in popularity, innovations in brewing techniques, flavoring, and product applications are shaping the future of this dynamic industry. This section explores cutting-edge developments in kombucha brewing, highlighting how these advancements are expanding the possibilities of kombucha both as a beverage and as a versatile product.

Advanced Fermentation Techniques

1. **Controlled Fermentation**: Technological advancements are allowing for more precise control over the fermentation process. Temperature-controlled fermentation chambers and automated pH monitoring systems enable brewers to consistently produce kombucha with desired flavor profiles and maintain quality control across batches.

2. **Hybrid Cultures**: Researchers and brewers are experimenting with hybrid SCOBYs that can ferment kombucha at different rates or with different flavor outcomes. These custom cultures can potentially reduce fermentation time and enhance specific health benefits or flavor notes.

3. **Alcohol Management**: Innovations in yeast management and fermentation processes are helping brewers more precisely control the alcohol content in kombucha, ensuring it remains below the legal threshold for non-alcoholic beverages while maximizing flavor and health benefits.

Novel Flavoring and Ingredients

1. **Exotic Flavors**: As global culinary trends influence kombucha brewing, exotic ingredients such as international fruits, rare herbs, and spices are being experimented with. This not only diversifies the flavor palette but also introduces new health benefits associated with these ingredients.

2. **Functional Additives**: The integration of functional ingredients such as vitamins, minerals, and adaptogens into kombucha is on the rise. These ingredients enhance the health-promoting properties of kombucha, appealing to health-conscious consumers looking for functional beverages.

3. **Collaborations with Other Beverages**: There is an increasing trend in cross-category innovations, such as kombucha-beer hybrids, kombucha-coffee blends, and kombucha-cocktails, which cater to diverse consumer preferences and occasions.

Sustainability and Production Efficiency

1. **Zero-Waste Production**: In response to growing environmental concerns, many kombucha producers are moving towards zero-waste operations. This includes finding uses for all by-products, such as creating distilled spirits from excess SCOBY, using waste tea leaves as compost, or developing edible SCOBY snacks.

2. **Energy-Efficient Brewing**: Advances in energy-efficient brewing equipment and practices are helping producers minimize their carbon footprint. Solar-powered brewing facilities and energy recovery systems are examples of how the industry is adopting more sustainable practices.

Packaging and Storage Innovations

1. **Smart Packaging**: The development of smart packaging technologies that can extend shelf life, monitor freshness, or display product information dynamically is becoming more

prevalent. These technologies can help reduce food waste and enhance consumer engagement.

2. **Eco-Friendly Materials**: There is a push towards more sustainable packaging options, such as biodegradable bottles or reusable containers, which not only appeal to environmentally conscious consumers but also help reduce the overall environmental impact of packaging.

Kombucha in Health and Wellness

1. **Targeted Health Formulas**: As research into the probiotic and biochemical properties of kombucha deepens, there is potential for developing targeted health formulas aimed at specific demographics or health concerns, such as digestive health, immune support, or even mood enhancement.

2. **Medical and Therapeutic Applications**: Preliminary research into kombucha's therapeutic properties could open doors for its use in more clinical or medicinal settings. This includes its potential role in managing diseases or in preventative health.

Innovation in kombucha brewing is driven by technological advancements, evolving consumer demands, and a growing emphasis on sustainability. As the industry continues to innovate, kombucha is set to become not only a staple health beverage but also a leader in the functional foods market. These developments promise exciting prospects for the future of kombucha, making it an ever-evolving field with vast potential.

Emerging Trends in Kombucha Consumption

As kombucha continues to evolve and expand its presence globally, emerging trends are shaping how and why consumers choose this fermented beverage. This section delves into the latest trends in kombucha consumption, highlighting shifts in consumer behavior, innovations in product offerings, and how these trends are influencing the market landscape.

Health-Conscious Consumers

1. **Functional Beverages**: The rise of health-conscious consumers continues to drive demand for beverages that offer more than just hydration. Kombucha is increasingly valued for its functional benefits, such as gut health support and immune system enhancement. This trend is prompting manufacturers to enhance their formulations with additional health-focused ingredients.

2. **Clean Label and Transparency**: Today's consumers are more informed and concerned about the ingredients in their beverages. There is a growing preference for products with clean labels—those with fewer, simpler ingredients. Kombucha producers are responding by ensuring their products are free from artificial additives and are clearly labeled with all ingredients.

Sustainability and Ethical Consumption

1. **Eco-Friendly Practices**: Consumers are increasingly making purchasing decisions based on environmental impact. Kombucha brands that adopt sustainable practices, such as using organic ingredients, sustainable packaging, and energy-efficient production processes, are gaining a competitive edge.

2. **Social Responsibility**: Alongside environmental concerns, social responsibility plays a crucial role in consumer choices. Kombucha companies that are involved in community building, fair trade practices, and supporting local economies are particularly appealing to modern consumers.

Personalization and Customization

1. **DIY Kombucha Kits**: As interest in personalized health and wellness grows, so does the trend toward DIY kombucha brewing. Consumers are eager to customize their kombucha

flavors and ingredients, leading to a rise in the popularity of home brewing kits and specialty supplies.

2. **Subscription Services**: Personalized subscription services that deliver kombucha directly to consumers' doors are becoming popular. These services often offer customization options for flavors or added functional ingredients, catering to individual preferences and dietary needs.

Technological Innovations

1. **Augmented Reality and Apps**: Some kombucha brands are incorporating augmented reality (AR) on their packaging to engage consumers with interactive content such as brewing tips, health information, and brand stories. Apps that track fermentation stages and flavor development are also enhancing the consumer experience.

2. **E-Commerce Growth**: Online sales channels for kombucha are expanding, fueled by improvements in distribution logistics that ensure products remain fresh during delivery. This trend is making kombucha more accessible to a wider audience.

New Consumption Contexts

1. **Kombucha in Culinary Contexts**: Beyond being a standalone drink, kombucha is making its way into the culinary world as an ingredient in recipes, ranging from salad dressings to marinades and even in desserts. This integration is part of a broader trend where traditional boundaries between food and drink categories are blurring.

2. **Kombucha Bars and Cafes**: Specialty kombucha bars and cafes are emerging as trendy destinations, similar to coffee shops and craft breweries. These venues often offer a variety of kombucha flavors on tap, kombucha cocktails, and other kombucha-infused products.

The future of kombucha consumption is shaped by a blend of health trends, technological advancements, and evolving consumer values, particularly around health, sustainability, and personalization. As these trends continue to develop, they will likely drive further innovation and growth in the kombucha industry, making kombucha a staple in diverse diets and lifestyles around the world.

Kombucha and Global Health Movements

Kombucha has become increasingly intertwined with global health movements, reflecting a broader shift towards more mindful consumption and wellness-oriented lifestyles. This section explores how kombucha is positioned within these movements and its potential impact on health trends around the world.

Aligning with Wellness Trends

1. **Holistic Health**: Kombucha is celebrated for its holistic health benefits, which align with the global trend towards integrative approaches to health and wellness. Consumers are increasingly seeking out natural, functional foods and beverages that support overall well-being, not just offer nutritional benefits. Kombucha fits this mold with its probiotic properties, potential detoxifying effects, and metabolic benefits.

2. **Preventative Health**: There is a growing emphasis on preventative health care, where diet plays a crucial role in maintaining health and preventing disease. Kombucha's purported immune-boosting and gut health-promoting properties make it a popular choice for those looking to enhance their diet with preventive health measures.

Sustainability and Health

1. **Eco-Conscious Consumption**: The global push towards sustainability has affected consumer choices significantly. Kombucha, particularly when produced with organic and locally

sourced ingredients, is seen as a sustainable beverage option. The fermentation process itself is energy-efficient and can be environmentally friendly, appealing to eco-conscious consumers.

2. **Low Waste Production**: Kombucha brewing, especially at a small or artisanal scale, typically generates less waste compared to mass-produced beverages. The SCOBY (Symbiotic Culture of Bacteria and Yeast) used in brewing can be reused many times, composted, or repurposed, which supports zero-waste lifestyles.

Global Health Advocacy

1. **Public Health Campaigns**: As part of efforts to combat the rise in lifestyle-related diseases, public health campaigns in various countries are promoting kombucha as a healthier alternative to sugary sodas and energy drinks. These initiatives often highlight kombucha's lower sugar content and beneficial enzymes and probiotics.

2. **Inclusion in Dietary Guidelines**: Some health advocacy groups are pushing for fermented foods like kombucha to be included in dietary guidelines, emphasizing their role in maintaining a healthy gut microbiome. This could potentially increase kombucha's visibility and consumption worldwide.

Cultural Integration and Adaptation

1. **Local Flavors and Ingredients**: As kombucha gains popularity globally, local brewers are experimenting with regional flavors and ingredients, creating unique versions of kombucha that reflect local tastes and culinary traditions. This not only helps in making kombucha more accessible but also integrates it into different cultural diets.

2. **Educational Outreach**: Organizations and health advocates are conducting workshops and seminars to educate the public about kombucha. These efforts often focus on how to brew kombucha at

home, understand its health benefits, and integrate it into daily diets.

Challenges and Opportunities

1. **Regulatory Challenges**: The classification and regulation of kombucha can vary significantly by country, affecting its marketing and consumption. Continued advocacy and education are necessary to navigate these regulatory landscapes effectively.

2. **Research and Development**: There is ongoing research into the health benefits of kombucha, which is crucial for its acceptance and integration into global health movements. More scientific backing is needed to support the health claims associated with kombucha, which could drive its inclusion in health policies and practices.

Kombucha's role in global health movements highlights its potential not just as a beverage but as a significant player in the larger narrative of health and wellness. As these trends evolve, kombucha could see enhanced integration into everyday health practices, supported by a growing body of research and a strong community of global consumers dedicated to health and sustainability.

Predictions and Possibilities

The future of kombucha appears robust and dynamic, influenced by evolving consumer preferences, technological advancements, and increasing global awareness of health and wellness. This section delves into predictions and possibilities for the growth and transformation of the kombucha market, exploring emerging trends and potential innovations that could shape its trajectory.

Continued Market Growth

1. **Global Expansion**: As awareness of kombucha grows, its market is expected to expand significantly, particularly in regions where it is currently less known. Markets in Asia, Latin America, and parts of Europe are likely to see considerable growth due to rising health consciousness and interest in fermented foods.

2. **Mainstream Acceptance**: Kombucha is predicted to transition from a niche health beverage to a mainstream option. This will be driven by larger beverage companies entering the kombucha market, increasing availability, and consumer interest in functional beverages.

Innovations in Flavor and Function

1. **Culinary Experimentation**: The diversity of kombucha flavors and formulations is expected to explode, with brewers experimenting with everything from exotic fruits and spices to CBD infusions. This innovation will cater to a broader range of tastes and dietary preferences.

2. **Functional Enhancements**: Kombucha products may increasingly incorporate additional functional ingredients, such as vitamins, minerals, and adaptogens. These enhancements will be designed to address specific health concerns like energy, relaxation, or immune support.

Technological Advancements

1. **Precision Fermentation**: Advances in biotechnology could lead to more precise control over the fermentation process, allowing for consistent production of kombucha with specific desired characteristics, such as exact probiotic counts or minimized alcohol levels.

2. **Packaging Innovations**: Smart packaging that can extend shelf life, monitor freshness, or even interact with consumers through embedded sensors and digital tags may become prevalent. This

technology could help in maintaining the quality of kombucha as it scales up and extends its distribution channels.

Sustainability Initiatives

1. **Eco-Friendly Production**: As sustainability becomes a significant factor in consumer purchasing decisions, kombucha companies will likely invest more in green production methods. This could include solar-powered breweries, water recycling systems, and waste reduction programs.

2. **Circular Economy Models**: There might be an increase in models that promote the circular use of resources, such as using spent tea leaves and other brewing by-products in new products, ranging from dietary supplements to cosmetic items.

Regulatory and Health Research Development

1. **Standardization of Regulations**: As kombucha becomes more globally recognized, there may be a move towards standardization of regulations concerning its production, labeling, and sale. This could help mitigate issues related to alcohol content, health claims, and consumer safety.

2. **Increased Research Investment**: With kombucha's rising popularity, there may be more significant investment in scientific research to substantiate health claims and explore new benefits. This could strengthen kombucha's position in the market as a health-promoting beverage.

The future of kombucha is not just promising but poised for transformation across various dimensions—market reach, product innovation, sustainability, and regulatory frameworks. As kombucha continues to evolve, it will likely integrate deeper into the dietary habits of global consumers, supported by a blend of tradition and innovation. The adaptability and enduring appeal of kombucha suggest that it will remain a significant player in the beverage industry for years to come.

APPENDICES

APPENDIX A: COMPARATIVE REVIEW OF KOMBUCHA BREWING KITS

For those interested in brewing kombucha at home, selecting the right brewing kit can significantly influence the ease and success of the brewing process. This section provides a comparative review of several popular kombucha brewing kits available on the market, focusing on features such as kit contents, ease of use, price, and customer reviews.

Kit Components Overview

Most kombucha brewing kits typically include the following components, though specific contents can vary:

1. **Glass Brewing Jar**: Essential for brewing and storing kombucha, sizes vary typically between 1 to 2 gallons.

2. **SCOBY (Symbiotic Culture of Bacteria and Yeast)**: Often accompanied by starter tea.

3. **Tea and Sugar**: Enough for the first batch or several batches.

4. **pH Test Strips**: To help maintain the proper acidity level during fermentation.

5. **Temperature Gauge**: Essential for monitoring the brewing environment.

6. **Covers and Rubber Bands**: For covering the jar during fermentation to keep out contaminants.

7. **Instructions**: Detailed guidelines to help beginners through the brewing process.

Key Kits in the Market

1. **The Kombucha Shop Kombucha Brewing Kit**

   - **Contents**: Includes a 1-gallon glass brew jar with plastic lid, organic kombucha culture and liquid starter tea, organic cane sugar, organic tea blend, reusable cotton tea bag, temperature gauge, cotton cover and rubber band, pH test strips, a pipette, a wet erase marker, step-by-step brewing instructions, and post-brewing guide.

   - **Ease of Use**: Excellent detailed instructions make this kit very beginner-friendly.

   - **Price**: Mid-range, offers good value considering the comprehensive nature of the kit.

   - **Customer Reviews**: Highly rated for the quality of ingredients and customer support.

2. **Craft a Brew Kombucha Starter Kit**

   - **Contents**: Features a 1-gallon glass brew jar, kombucha culture (SCOBY), tea steeping bag, organic black tea, organic cane sugar, thermometer, and elastic cloth cover.

   - **Ease of Use**: Simple and straightforward, suitable for beginners.

   - **Price**: On the lower end, making it a budget-friendly option.

   - **Customer Reviews**: Generally positive, though some users noted needing additional resources for troubleshooting.

3. **Fermentaholics The Complete Kombucha Brewing Kit**

   - **Contents**: This kit includes USDA organic SCOBY with pre-measured starter tea, 1-gallon brew jar, tea blend, organic cane sugar, reusable cotton tea bag, pipette, adhesive thermometer strip, cotton cloth cover, detailed instructions, rubber band, and pH strips.

- **Ease of Use**: Well-documented instructions with access to online support resources.

- **Price**: Mid-range, competitive for the quality and organic certifications.

- **Customer Reviews**: Excellent, especially for the health and responsiveness of the SCOBY and the inclusion of organic ingredients.

Choosing the right kombucha brewing kit depends on personal preferences, budget, and brewing ambitions. For beginners, kits with detailed instructions and responsive customer support are recommended. Those more experienced may prioritize kits with higher capacities or specific features like continuous brewing systems. All the reviewed kits provide the essentials needed to start brewing kombucha at home successfully, with variations mostly in additional features and quality of components. As home brewing continues to gain popularity, these kits serve as a gateway to mastering the art and science of kombucha making.

APPENDIX B: COMPREHENSIVE GLOSSARY OF ESSENTIAL KOMBUCHA TERMS

1. Acetic Acid

Definition: A primary acid produced during the fermentation of kombucha, contributing to its characteristic sour taste. Acetic acid also has preservative qualities, helping to inhibit the growth of harmful bacteria.

2. Aerobic Fermentation

Definition: Fermentation that occurs in the presence of oxygen. In kombucha brewing, this specifically refers to the bacteria converting alcohol into acetic acid, which happens when the fermenting tea is exposed to air.

3. Anaerobic Fermentation

Definition: Fermentation that occurs without the presence of oxygen. In kombucha, this primarily involves the yeast breaking down sugars into alcohol and carbon dioxide.

4. Antioxidants

Definition: Molecules that inhibit the oxidation of other molecules. Antioxidants in kombucha, primarily derived from its tea base, help prevent cell damage and offer various health benefits, including anti-inflammatory properties.

5. Batch

Definition: Refers to a specific quantity of kombucha brewed at one time under the same conditions. A batch begins with the mixing of tea, sugar, and starter culture and ends with the completion of the primary fermentation.

6. Batch Brewing

Definition: A method where kombucha is made in distinct batches. Each batch starts with a combination of sweet tea and starter liquid and undergoes a complete fermentation cycle before being processed or consumed.

7. Clarification

Definition: The process by which suspended particles in kombucha settle or are filtered out, resulting in a clearer beverage. Clarification can occur naturally over time or be expedited by cold temperatures or filtration methods.

8. Continuous Brew

Definition: A method of brewing kombucha where fresh sweetened tea is added to a portion of mature kombucha in a continuous cycle, as opposed to starting from scratch each time. This method is favored for its convenience and the more consistent supply of kombucha it provides.

9. Continuous Brewing

Definition: A brewing method where tea and sugar are periodically added to a portion of mature kombucha while continuously drawing off the fermented drink. This system is often used to maintain a constant supply of kombucha.

10. Cross-Contamination

Definition: The unintentional transfer of bacteria, yeasts, or other microorganisms from one substance or object to another, with potentially harmful effects. In kombucha brewing, maintaining strict hygiene practices is crucial to prevent cross-contamination and ensure a healthy fermentation process.

11. Culture

Definition: In microbiology, a culture is the cultivation of microorganisms in a controlled environment. In kombucha, "culture" refers to the SCOBY, which contains the bacteria and yeast necessary for fermentation.

12. Detoxification

Definition: In the context of health and wellness, detoxification refers to the process of removing toxic substances from the body. Kombucha is often claimed to support detoxification due to its acids and enzymes that may help cleanse the liver.

13. Ethanol

Definition: A type of alcohol produced by yeast during the fermentation process. In kombucha, ethanol is further converted into acetic acid by bacteria, contributing to the beverage's tartness.

14. F1 and F2

Definition: Abbreviations for "First Fermentation" and "Second Fermentation." F1 refers to the primary fermentation process where the SCOBY digests the sugar. F2 is an optional secondary fermentation used to enhance flavor and carbonation, often involving the addition of fruit juices, herbs, or other flavorings.

15. Fermentation

Definition: A metabolic process that produces chemical changes in organic substrates through the action of enzymes. In the context of kombucha, it refers to the process by which SCOBY converts sugar into ethanol and acetic acid.

16. Fermenter

Definition: The container or vessel used for fermenting kombucha. It must be non-reactive and clean, typically made of glass or food-grade plastic, to prevent any unwanted chemical reactions or contamination.

17. Flavoring

Definition: The process of adding additional ingredients such as fruits, herbs, or spices to kombucha during the second fermentation (F2) to enhance its taste. Flavoring not only improves the beverage's palatability but also can add to its health benefits.

18. Functional Beverages

Definition: Drinks that contain ingredients with potential health benefits beyond basic nutritional value. Kombucha is categorized as a functional beverage due to its probiotic content and associated health benefits.

19. Hydrometer

Definition: A tool used to measure the specific gravity or relative density of liquids in relation to water. In kombucha brewing, a hydrometer can help monitor the progress of fermentation by measuring sugar content.

20. Infusion

Definition: The process of extracting flavors and nutrients from plant materials by steeping them in liquid. In the case of kombucha, infusion typically refers to the steeping of tea leaves to prepare the tea base before adding the SCOBY.

21. Kombucha

Definition: A fermented tea beverage that originates from Northeast China around 220 B.C. It is known for its slightly sour and fizzy characteristics, which result from the fermentation process.

22. Mother Culture

Definition: Another term for SCOBY, specifically referring to the original culture from which subsequent kombuchas are brewed. The mother culture is the source of the bacteria and yeast necessary for fermentation.

23. Pellicle

Definition: The cellulose mat that forms on top of the kombucha during fermentation, often seen as a sign of active fermentation. This layer is created by bacteria as part of the SCOBY.

24. Pellicle Formation

Definition: The process by which a new cellulose layer forms on the surface of kombucha during fermentation, often seen as a sign of active fermentation. This layer is created by bacteria as part of the SCOBY.

25. pH Level

Definition: A measure of how acidic or basic a liquid is. Kombucha typically has a pH between 2.5 and 3.5 at the end of fermentation, which is mildly acidic.

26. Preservation

Definition: In kombucha, preservation refers to the ability of the beverage to remain safe and palatable over time. The acidic nature of kombucha acts as a natural preservative, helping to prevent the growth of harmful microorganisms.

27. Probiotics

Definition: Live microorganisms that are intended to have health benefits when consumed or applied to the body. Kombucha is valued for its probiotic content, particularly the beneficial bacteria that can aid in digestion and overall gut health.

28. SCOBY

Definition: An acronym for Symbiotic Culture Of Bacteria and Yeast. This is the living culture used to ferment sweet tea into kombucha. It appears as a gelatinous, pancake-like disc that floats on the surface of the kombucha during fermentation.

29. Secondary Fermentation

Definition: An optional but common stage in kombucha brewing where the fermented tea undergoes a second fermentation phase in a sealed bottle, often with added flavorings. This stage enhances carbonation and flavor complexity.

30. Starter Tea

Definition: Previously brewed kombucha or a vinegar solution used to initiate the fermentation process of a new batch of kombucha. It helps to acidify the brew, preventing harmful bacteria from proliferating.

31. Symbiosis

Definition: A mutually beneficial relationship between different organisms. In kombucha, symbiosis occurs between bacteria and yeast within the SCOBY, where each provides essential nutrients or environmental conditions needed by the other.

32. Tannins

Definition: Naturally occurring compounds found in tea leaves. Tannins contribute to the flavor profile of kombucha and affect its clarity and color. They also provide nutrients essential for the growth of the SCOBY.

33. Trace Elements

Definition: Small quantities of minerals required by the human body for proper health, which are naturally present in kombucha. These include zinc, copper, iron, and manganese, which can contribute to various metabolic processes.

34. Yeast

Definition: Microorganisms that are part of the fungi kingdom. In kombucha brewing, yeast plays a crucial role by converting the sugars in tea to alcohol and carbon dioxide, initiating the fermentation process.

APPENDIX C: RESOURCE LIST FOR FURTHER EXPLORATION AND SUPPLIES

Delving deeper into the world of kombucha brewing requires access to reliable resources and quality supplies. Whether you are a beginner looking to start your first batch or an experienced brewer seeking to refine your craft, this section provides a curated list of resources and suppliers that can help you on your kombucha journey.

Books and Publications

1. **"The Big Book of Kombucha" by Hannah Crum & Alex LaGory**

   - Comprehensive guide to brewing kombucha, understanding the science behind it, and exploring the variety of ways it can be used.

2. **"Kombucha Revolution" by Stephen Lee with Ken Koopman**

   - Focuses on innovative recipes and uses for kombucha, including cocktails, smoothies, and other creative culinary applications.

3. **"The Art of Fermentation" by Sandor Ellix Katz**

   - While not solely about kombucha, this book provides an in-depth look at fermentation processes, including detailed information on fermenting teas.

Online Forums and Communities

1. **Everything Kombucha Facebook Group**

- Link: facebook.com/groups/everythingkombucha/
- The official Facebook group for the Everything Kombucha brand where anybody can join and share their favorite kombucha teas, recipes, articles, guides, experiences, infographics, and any & all helpful kombucha knowledge.

2. **Kombucha Kamp**

- Website: kombuchakamp.com
- A hub for all things kombucha, including tutorials, troubleshooting tips, and supplies. They also have an active online community.

3. **Reddit – r/Kombucha**

- Link: reddit.com/r/Kombucha/
- A subreddit dedicated to kombucha enthusiasts where brewers share experiences, advice, and recipes.

4. **Home Brew Talk – Kombucha & Fermented Tea Forum**

- Website: homebrewtalk.com
- A forum for discussions on home brewing, including a section specifically for kombucha and other fermented teas.

Suppliers of Kombucha Brewing Equipment and Ingredients

1. **Kombucha Brooklyn**

- Website: kombuchabrooklyn.com
- Supplies everything from starter kits to ingredients and brewing equipment tailored for kombucha production.

2. **Cultures for Health**

- Website: culturesforhealth.com
- Offers a range of products for fermenting at home, including kombucha starter cultures, brewing vessels, and flavoring agents.

3. **Oregon Kombucha**

- Website: oregonkombucha.com
- Provides organic kombucha starter kits and a variety of tea blends specifically chosen for brewing kombucha.

Online Courses and Workshops

1. **Udemy – Kombucha Brewing Masterclass**

- A comprehensive online course that covers the basics of kombucha brewing as well as advanced techniques and flavoring.

2. **Kombucha Brewers International**

- Website: kombuchabrewers.org
- Offers webinars and workshops on kombucha brewing, industry trends, and business practices related to kombucha.

YouTube Channels

1. **You Brew Kombucha**

- Provides detailed DIY videos on kombucha brewing, from the basics to more advanced techniques, including troubleshooting common issues.

2. **Booch and Brew**

- Offers a mix of instructional videos on kombucha brewing and insights into the culture and science behind the fermentation process.

ABOUT THE AUTHOR

Jeffrey Ito is a seasoned kombucha enthusiast and author with a background in Industrial & Systems Engineering from the University of Southern California. His journey into kombucha brewing began over a decade ago during his college years when he discovered the unique flavors and health benefits of fermented foods. Since then, Jeffrey has mastered kombucha brewing, combining his engineering expertise with his passion for nutrition and sustainable living.

Dedicated to sharing his knowledge, Jeffrey conducts workshops, writes insightful articles, and speaks at conferences to promote kombucha as a healthful and sustainable choice. In his book, he offers practical brewing tips, favorite recipes, and insights into kombucha's cultural significance, aiming to demystify the process and inspire others to explore kombucha brewing. When not engaged with kombucha, Jeffrey enjoys hiking and continuing his education in health and sustainability.

Printed in Great Britain
by Amazon